Keto Meal Prep Cookbook for Beginners

The Easy-to-Follow Meal Prep Guide for Keto Diet Beginners with 16 Weeks Meal Plans to Live Better

Eric Baker

Table of Content

Introduction

Speaking of the keto experience, there are tons of articles, blogs and books that tell you how easy and super awesome this low-carb, sugar-free dietary approach is to follow. But rare are the few who tell you how to cope with the challenges that come when you transition into the keto

lifestyle. For most of us, a high carb diet is the only reality our body has ever dealt with, so to switch to a keto lifestyle is a great challenge in itself. What I recommend to all beginners or anyone who is struggling to make such a change is to start from the basics and work your way up the ladder. Set one milestone at a time and gradually move to the next. And just when you start feeling like you can cut off carbs and sugars from the diet- just go for the big leap!

I am glad that you have decided to be a part of our one big keto family. Being on this journey can make you hit several bumps on the way, but with the right approach and complete understanding of the diet, it gets a little less challenging every day.

The early phase of the ketogenic transition is always the hardest and what helped me the most during those days were my meal planning and prepping skills. Following a ketogenic diet plan, or any other dietary approach for that matter, requires a certain level of discipline and organization; and meal prepping is all about doing that. When you have a pre-made meal stored in your refrigerator ready to be served, then it gets a little easier to stay away from all the temptations.

So here I am, summing up my very own keto meal prepping experience into this cookbook. There are a lot of delicious, highly nutritious and low-carb meal ideas I shared in here that you can prepare ahead of time and store on a weekly or monthly basis. Besides those recipes, what you need are some basics about the ketogenic diet, the methods of meal prepping and a weekly meal plan, especially if you are a beginner, to get started with your very own keto experience. So, here comes all you need to know about the ketogenic meal prepping approach with an interesting collection of recipes along with a 16 weeks comprehensive meal plan.

Chapter 1 Getting To Know The Ketogenic Diet

The ketogenic diet is a low-carb, high fat and moderate protein intake approach which focuses on limiting the carb intake to kick start a metabolic process called "ketosis" in the body. To achieve that, the average daily consumption of carbs has to be less than 50 grams. A ketogenic diet must contain 55-60 per cent fat, 30- 35 per cent protein, and 5-10 per cent carbohydrates, so it has to be free from all the grains, legumes, tubers, sugars, and starchy vegetables and fruits. That may seem a lot to cut down from your diet, but there is a whole list of substitutes that you can incorporate into your diet to make it healthy, nutritious and full of flavors and my extensive ketogenic meal prep recipes collection is a testament of that. Before going to the recipes, let's dig a little deeper into the diet and see how it works and what it calls for.

How Does The Ketogenic Diet Work?

Ketosis! that's how the ketogenic diet works to make your body healthier. Ketosis is a naturally occurring process that the body initiates whenever the blood glucose levels start dropping to the lowest levels. In order to get energy for the working of the cells and organs, the body goes into ketosis, in which the fat molecules are metabolized to release the required amount of energy. The type of energy released from the fats is much higher than that derived from carbohydrates, and it is more long-lasting. The ketosis only lasts when the blood glucose levels are low, and there is no amount of sufficient carbohydrates provided to the body during that time.

The ketogenic diet is created to deliberately kick start ketosis in the body and achieve the many great benefits of this process- which mainly includes fat burning, aka weight loss. That is why the ketogenic diet is often branded as a weight loss program. However, the perks of living on a low-carb diet go beyond that. You see, the word ketosis comes from the ketones which are produced by the liver when it metabolizes fats to produce energy. The release of ketones is linked to several other health benefits.

What to Expect?

The ketogenic diet is largely branded as a perfect weight loss plan as if it only works to counter obesity. But this diet and the ketosis together bring several health-transformational changes to the body, and that all works to counter many diseases and reverse a few.

Weight Loss: The ability to lose weight quickly is one of the main advantages of the ketogenic diet. When you restrict carbohydrates to the point where you're in ketosis, you'll see a considerable reduction in body fat as well as an increase or retention of muscle mass.

Restores Insulin Sensitivity: A ketogenic diet has been demonstrated to help in the restoration of insulin sensitivity by removing the core cause of insulin resistance, which is excessive insulin levels in the body. Because minimal carbohydrate intake means low insulin, this diet helps in the maintenance of low insulin levels. A high-carbohydrate diet adds fuel to the fire of insulin resistance. It necessitates more insulin, which exacerbates insulin resistance.

Lowers High Blood Pressure: A ketogenic diet has been found in several studies to lower blood pressure in patients who are overweight or have type 2 diabetes.

Improves Mental Health: Other common reported benefits of a ketogenic diet include mental clarity, enhanced ability to focus, and improved memory. Increasing your consumption of omega-3 fats, such as those found in oily fish like salmon, tuna, and mackerel, will help you feel better and learn better. This is because omega-3 boosts the amount of DHA, a fatty acid that forms approximately 15 to 30% of our brain. Long-term memory performance is aided by the formation of beta-hydroxybutyrate, a type of ketone.

*Keto Flu

People experience a set of symptoms during the first seven days or so after switching to the Ketogenic diet, which is termed as keto flu. The symptoms include frequent headaches, fatigue, foggy brain, nausea, irritability, difficulty sleeping, and constipation. Keto flu is only temporary, and it only represents the great transition your body goes through when it starts running on ketosis. The symptoms usually last for a week or two. Staying hydrated and active can help get rid of the symptoms earlier than expected.

Things to Eat

If you are planning to go, Keto, you will have to turn into a carb-repellent. That's right, look out for anything carb-rich and keep it out of your kitchen, pantry and refrigerator. Here is the list of ingredients that are considered keto-friendly, and you can use them in your diet freely:

All-Protein Meals: Whether it is seafood, poultry, beef, lamb meat or pork, as long as these meats are not cooked with high-carb ingredients, they are great for your ketogenic diet. Similarly, ingredients like tofu, tempeh or seitan, which are also termed vegan meats, are also a great way to add proteins to your ketogenic meals.

Dairy Is Good: All dairy product except animal milk is great for the ketogenic diet. The reason is the high carbohydrate level in the milk, which is not the case with the cream, yogurt, cream cheese and cheese as these products have higher fat to carbs ratio. Instead of milk, you can go for carb-free plant-based milk like unsweetened almond milk, coconut milk or soy milk etc.

Starch Free Vegetables: Vegetables which do not have excessive carbs are the healthiest addition to the ketogenic menu. All green leaves, the herbs, the aromatics like onion, celery, carrots and any other vegetable other than starchy tubers, and some squashes are great to keep your meal low-carb.

Fats Are The Best: Ketogenic is, in fact, a low-carb and high-fat diet, so any form of edible fat is considered suitable for this dietary plan. From butter to vegetable oils, you can add them all to your diet.

Nuts and Seeds: Adding seeds and nuts to a meal sure makes it nutri-dense. They are low in carbs and high in essential oils.

Low-Carb Fruits: Since most fruits are rich in sugars, they don't make a good addition to the ketogenic diet. Only berries and avocado qualify as keto-friendly fruits.

Keto Substitutes: Since most high carb ingredients are restricted on the ketogenic diet, their keto-friendly substitutes must be used in different recipes. Low-carb keto substitutes include:

- **Flour:** coconut flour and almond flour

- **Sweeteners:** stevia, erythritol, swerve, monk fruit sweetener.

- **Milk:** coconut milk, almond milk, hemp milk, soy milk

Commonly Used Condiments

For the commonly used condiments of oil, salt, soy sauce and vinegar, as well as dry food materials that can be preserved for a long time, it is completed at the first purchase, and then the weekly shopping list is down to the purchase of fresh food materials.

Flour	Condiments		
Almond flour	Salt	Italian seasoning	Shichimi seasoning
Coconut flour	Sea salt	Cajun seasoning	Taco seasoning mix
Cocoa powder	Black pepper	Tamari	Dried parsley
Baking powder	Dijon mustard	Erythritol	Ground cinnamon
Baking soda	Yellow mustard	Paprika	Sun-dried tomatoes
Whey protein powder	Garlic	Chili paste	Mixed herbs
	Garlic powder	Chili powder	Mint leaves
	Dried basil	Lemon juice	Low-carb marinara
	Dried oregano	Lemon juice extract	sauce
	Dried dill weed		Steak sauce
	Dried thyme		

Fats	Dairy	Vinegar and Wine	Nut and Seeds
Olive oil	Cheddar cheese	Vodka	Pumpkin seeds
Extra-virgin olive oil	Parmesan cheese	Xanthan gum vinegar	Sunflower seeds
Coconut oil	Mozzarella cheese	White wine vinegar	Fennel seeds
Refined avocado oil	Cream cheese	White wine	Chia seeds
	Goat cheese	Dry white wine	White sesame seeds
	Sugar-free tomato sauce	Balsamic vinegar	Black sesame seeds
	Heavy cream	Apple cider vinegar	Hemp seeds
	Vanilla extract	Red wine vinegar	Poppy seeds
	Butter	Keto-friendly mayonnaise	Sunflower seeds
			Fennel seeds
			Walnuts

Things to Avoid

Remember, the aim is to keep the carb intake less than 5-10 per cent in every meal. And that is impossible to achieve if you will consume the following carb-rich ingredients. They are therefore restricted on the ketogenic diet.

1. Grains have a high proportion of carbs; that is why you don't find wheat, flour, rice and other grains being used in ketogenic recipes. Food like crackers, cereal, rice, bread, pasta, and beer all carry a high amount of carbs, and hence they should be avoided. Carbohydrates are abundant in whole-wheat pasta and bean-based pasta. Rely on nuts based flours to make bread and other baked goods. Instead of grain pasta, you can try spiralized zucchini and carrots to make some noodles.

2. Beans and legumes are high in fibre and protein, making them heart-healthy food, but they are also high in carbs. This group of food contains red beans, white, pinto, garbanzo, chickpeas, black, and cannellini beans, split peas and all sorts of legumes.

3. Starchy vegetables such as beets, potatoes, corn, and sweet potatoes should be avoided because they contain more digestible carbohydrates than fibre. Similarly, high-sugar fruits, except berries and avocados, contain more carbohydrates and should also be avoided.

4. A single cup of milk contains 12 grams of lactose which is sugar, so you can not use it in your meals. Instead, use almond, coconut, or similar low-carb milk.

5. To keep added sugars to a minimum, stick to plain yoghurt. Greek yoghurt contains more protein and fewer carbs than ordinary yoghurt.

6. Fruit juice, whether natural or not, is strong in quick-digesting carbohydrates that cause blood sugar levels to surge. So don't drink it.

7. Sugar, honey, maple syrup, and other sweets are heavy in carbs and poor in nutrients, so avoid them.

8. Chips, crackers, and other grain-based foods are high in carbs but low in fibre.

9. Gluten-free does not imply that the products are carb-free. In fact, many gluten-free breads and muffins have the same amount of carbs as regular baked items. They are generally deficient in fibre as well.

Chapter 2 Meal Prep Helps!

When you have to follow a dietary approach as strict as the ketogenic diet, meal prep really helps. As I said earlier, this new healthier lifestyle of yours is going to require discipline, and that's what meal prepping brings to you. You prepare the ingredients, cook them ahead and store

them to serve ready-to-eat meals at the table. Meal prepping works for everyone, whether you are working outside, at home or taking care of the kids. With all that is going on in your busy life, meal prepping can really make you stick to the diet you want to follow. That is why I always recommend meal prepping to the Keto and the Non-keto dieters, and here is why you should go for it:

Why Should You Meal Prep?

At first, meal preparation may appear to be a weekend hassle, but after you hear about the numerous advantages that this healthy culinary practice has to offer, you won't be able to resist giving it a try. The vast majority of people who use meal prep to enjoy a nutritious home-cooked meals today say it has helped them in analyzing their eating patterns and forcing them to change when they are found to be unhealthy. Let's take a look at why meal planning is so important in today's society, especially when life moves at a faster pace than we can imagine.

♦ It Saves Money and Time

In a tight schedule, no one has time to think or prepare food, and cooking is practically impossible. The only other option is to order food and eat it somewhere. That is always more expensive and harmful than pre-cooking a meal at home. You have more time to analyze the cost and quality of the ingredients you bring home when you plan and prepare dinner in your leisure time. Meal planning saves your money by preventing you from buying unnecessary kitchen items.

Even though meal planning takes up some of your free time on weekends, which is obvious as you will be preparing the complete menu for the next few days in one day, however, this additional time investment will save your time during the weekdays. You won't have to think about cooking or preparing a whole meal after a long day at work. You may easily reheat and serve food that has been stored in your refrigerator. You will not have to do any cleaning or dishwashing after every meal. That's how meal prep can help you make the most of your time.

♦ It Makes Grocery Shopping Easier

Grocery shopping becomes a mess when you go into the store with no idea what you need and no plan in mind. It's a waste of time and energy to walk around a store looking for something and buying things you may or may not need. When it comes to meal preparation, on the other hand, you have a short and well-organized grocery list in hand, and all you have to do now is get the exact items and check out. That's how meal planning makes grocery shopping a breeze.

♦ It Keeps You Motivated

It is never easy to follow a healthy lifestyle or to stick to a health-oriented diet plan. People give up quickly when they lose all their motivation and willpower. Meal prep can help you achieve that much-needed consistency. You will be able to stick to this routine without losing the desire to eat if you cook and store all of the nutritious meals in your refrigerator according to a fixed menu and schedule. And once meal prep is put into reality, it boosts a person's motivation even more.

How to Meal Prep?

Meal prepping may seem an extra weight added to your already busy routine, but with better management of time and resources, you can reap its true benefits. You get better at it with time and experience. I suggest to breakdown the whole process into a few simple steps and then accomplish each one after another.

Step 01: Make an Organized Grocery List

Make a precise grocery list organized by supermarket categories to save time at the grocery store. You'll save time by not having to go back to a prior section, and you'll be able to finish your buying faster. Limiting your grocery shopping trip to once a week can save more of your time.

Step 02: Manage Cooking Time

A good working flow while cooking in the kitchen always saves a significant amount of time. Start with the recipe with the longest cooking time to manage the prep and cook times of other recipes. Prepare the ingredients of other recipes when one is already cooking on the stove. Cold dishes like salad dressing or salads should be prepared last because they can be prepared while the other dishes are cooking. To save more of your time, you can make use of all the cooking appliances at once. Cook one meal in the oven, another on the stove; try cooking one in the air fryer, in a pressure cooker and in the rice cooker.

Step 03: Cook Make-ahead Meals

You can prepare meals that can be refrigerated and reheated at a later time. This is especially useful for evening meals. You can cook large batches of food and then divide them into individual portions to store for different days of the week.

Step 04: Store Properly

Another crucial step is to select the appropriate container. The container should be the same size as the serving size of the meal you plan to eat later. The sort of container or storage is another something to think about. Store liquids such as soups, broths, and smoothies in glass jars or boxes. To keep veggies, fruits, tofu, and other dry solid foods fresh, use bee wraps or plastic bags. You may easily manage the space within your refrigerator by using different storage containers, and it becomes easier to reheat the food for each serving.

Storage Essentials

Without the right tools and ingredients, meal prep is impossible. To prepare a large number of meals in a short period, we require additional assistance in the shape of appropriate kitchen materials. Even before going food shopping, a person should get the following kitchen items to make the best meal prep meals. The things on this list helps in speedy cooking, make storage easier and more convenient for all serving sizes and food quantities, and aid in preparing a weekly meal schedule.

1. Food Prepping Tools

It's crucial to have a good chopper, food processor, dicer, or spiralizer on hand when you're doing your meal prep. Because there are a variety of products available, you can select the most effective and efficient one. When it comes to meal prep, electric choppers and mixers can be useful.

2. Sealable Jars

To keep liquid foods such as cooked soups, stews, broths, pickles, poached vegetables, and fruits, glass mason jars or canning jars with sealable lids are ideal. These jars come in a range of forms and sizes and are readily available in supermarkets. Choose jars that are appropriate for your serving size and amount. Alternatively, you can buy a set of mason jars in various sizes to match your needs. When the jars are filled with food, they should be clean, sterilized- preferably, and sealed. To prevent the food from being contaminated, the lid should be tightly secured.

3. Eco-Friendly Food Wraps

This bee's food wrap is ideal for covering and storing food in the fridge. This wrap is ideal for storing a meal for the same day or the following day when the items that cannot be stored in a sealed container.

4. Glass-lock Storage Containers

Glass containers work wonders when it comes to food storage. They are chemical and BPA free, so there is no chance of contamination, unlike plastic containers. You can reheat the dish in the microwave without changing the container. Glass lock containers are available in a wide range of sizes and shapes.

5. Reusable Storage Food Bags

Food should not be stored in plastic bags. They are a persistent source of microplastic and chemical pollutants that progressively seeps into our food. Instead of using plastic bags, use reusable silicone food bags, which are both chemical and plastic-free. They can withstand pressure and are temperature resistant when layered. Food doesn't stick to the bags' walls, and they're machine washable. A silicone bag can last for months without losing its effectiveness. These bags are both affordable and practical.

6. Label What You Store

Most of the time, if you don't name meals stored, you'll get disoriented. It's difficult to remember what you ate each day and what you've placed in a specific container. To avoid any mistakes, write the recipe name as well as the day and time for serving on small paper notes, stick them on the respective containers, and then store them. Even if the food is frozen, the label can aid in meal identification. Place the stored food in the proper serving sequence. Keep the containers according to the order of their serving date.

Food Storage Chart

Meat	FRIDGE	FREEZER
Salads: Egg Salad, Tuna Salad Chicken	3 To 5 Days	Does Not Freeze Well
Hamburger, Meatloaf, And Other Dishes Made With Ground Meat (Raw)	1 To 2 Days	3 To 4 Months
Steaks: Beef, Lamb Pork, (Raw)	3 To 5 Days	3 To 4 Months
Chops: Beef, Lamb Pork, (Raw)	3 To 5 Days	4 To 6 Months
Roasts: Beef, Lamb Pork, (Raw)	3 To 5 Days	4 To 12 Months
Whole Chicken Turkey Or, (Raw)	1 To 2 Days	1 Year
Pieces: Chicken Turkey Or, (Raw)	1 To 2 Days	9 Months
Soups And Stews With Vegetables And Meat	3 To 4 Days	2 To 3 Months
Pizza	3 To 5 Days	1 To 2 Months
Beef, Lamb Pork, Or Chicken (Cooked)	3 To 5 Days	2 To 6 Months

FRESH MEATS	FRIDGE	FREEZER
Salads, Eggs, Fish	1 To 2 Days	Does Not Freeze Well
Beef, Pork, Lamb	1 To 2 Days	3 To 4 Months
Bacon	7 Days	1 Month
Poultry	1 To 2 Days	9 To 12 Months

COOKED MEATS	FRIDGE	FREEZER
Salads, Eggs, Fish	3 To 5 Days	Does Not Freeze Well
Beef, Pork, Lamb	3 To 5 Days	3 To 6 Months (Up To 12 Months For Roasts)
Bacon	7 Days	1 Month
Poultry	3 To 5 Days	2 To 4 Months

Smart Meal Prepping Tips

Storage is the most integral part of meal prepping; no matter how good food you cook, that food will be of no use without putting extra effort into the storage. Meal prepping is all about learning the effective methods of storage, and here are some simple tips that can help you store all types of food efficiently.

* Start Small

If you're new to meal prepping, it can be intimidating. Start gently and create one or two recipes your first week, rather than attempting to prepare a week's worth of food in one day. Choose one day of the week to do all of the cooking, and when you get the hang of it, you can increase the amount of food you prepare.

* Keep Storage Space Organized

Another key aspect of meal preparation is keeping the storage area neat and clean. For our convenience, both the refrigerator and the freezer must be nicely arranged. It is preferable to store different types of meals in different compartments of the refrigerator. For example, you may divide the areas into sections based on days or mealtimes, such as one portion for breakfast only, another for lunch, one for snacks, and another for the evening. This categorization of the saved meals will make it easier to find the meal at the right time without having to think too hard about it.

* Make a Meal Schedule

It's critical to have a plan when meal prepping; otherwise, there's no point. You should schedule when you'll consume the meals you're preparing ahead of time. You might, for example, have vegetarian Mondays and Taco Tuesdays. The plan must be practical, and it should have such a combination of meals in a day that all your nutritional needs are met every day. It is best to mix and match different recipes to keep your menu a little interesting every day. Keep your food preferences in consideration while making this schedule.

* Check the Expiry Date

You can reduce the chances of food spoilage by purchasing food products with the earliest Expiration Date. Any meal containing such a product should be easily stored in the refrigerator for a longer period of time if the expiry date gives you a margin of 2-3 weeks. The expiration date of dairy products should be carefully examined.

* Never Pack Hot Food

When you transfer the freshly cooked meal to a container and cover it, it may trap the moisture inside, which may lead to early spoilage. Let your meal cool down to room temperature, and then transfer it to the designated container. Divide your meal prep time into three parts: cooking first, then allowing all of the food to cool, and last, dividing the prepared food into serving portions in the containers.

* Make Freezer-friendly Meals

You may have everything from keto lasagna and casseroles to a substantial beef stew ready to go if you take the time to prepare these freezer-friendly recipes ahead of time. The secret is to defrost these ready-to-eat meals well before you want to eat them.

* Make Use of Jar For Salads

You can prepare enough jar salads to last a few days if you have the correct ingredients on hand. Layer the different salad ingredients in a mason jar and eat with a fork at lunchtime. However, you must stack your ingredients appropriately to keep your salad fresh and crisp. The salad dressing must be added to the bottom, then place the meat on top. Add your veggies, cheese, and lettuce to finish off the salad.

Conclusion

With that many recipes and a very own ketogenic meal prepping meal plan, you don't need to rely on anyone to give that first push. Now you just need to pick up just the right ingredients and put them together to make a wide variety of low-carb meals. And that is what I ever wanted- a comprehensive ketogenic meal prep guide that could help everyone, especially the beginners, to start their keto journey the right way.

Chapter 3 Meal Plans and Recipes

Guess what? I threw together four meal prep plans to help you get started on this whole thing. They do all those wonderful things we've talked about thus far from repurposing ingredients to fit multiple meals to mixing and matching with several keto delicious sides. I make and eat these recipes often in my own household, and they each have the added benefit of being absolutely delectable. I hope you'll give them a try!

Prep Plan #1

Meal Plan	Breakfast	Lunch	Dinner
Day-1	Mushroom Cheese Frittata	Bacon Salad with Feta Cheese	(Not Keto)
Day-2	(Not Keto)	Easy Air Fryer Lemon Chicken	Garlicky Mushrooms and Spinach Italian Style
Day-3	Avocado Eggs with Spicy Sauce (Plan #3)	(Not Keto)	Bacon Salad with Feta Cheese
Day-4	(Not Keto)	Garlicky Mushrooms and Spinach Italian Style	Easy Air Fryer Lemon Chicken
Day-5	Mushroom Cheese Frittata	Bacon Salad with Feta Cheese	(Not Keto)
Day-6	(Not Keto)	Easy Air Fryer Lemon Chicken	Garlicky Mushrooms and Spinach Italian Style
Day-7	Avocado Eggs with Spicy Sauce (Plan #3)	(Not Keto)	Bacon Salad with Feta Cheese

Shopping List

* Eggs
* Mushrooms
* Two 4 oz pack of cheese
* One 12 oz pack of bacon
* Leafy greens
* Spinach
* 4 skin-on, bone-in chicken thighs

* Sun-dried tomatoes
* Scallions
* Feta cheese
* Parsley
* 2 heads of garlic
* Basil leaves
* 4 lemon wedges

Mushroom Cheese Frittata

Bacon Salad with Feta Cheese

Garlicky Mushrooms and Spinach Italian Style

Easy Air Fryer Lemon Chicken

Recipe 1 (Breakfast): Mushroom Cheese Frittata | Fat 86% | Protein 12% | Carbs 2%

Makes: 4 servings **Prep time:** 15 minutes **Store:** In an airtight container in the fridge for up to 4 days or in the freezer for up to 1 month.

VINAIGRETTE:
4 tbsps. olive oil
1 tbsp. white wine vinegar
FRITTATA:
1 pound (454 g) sliced mushrooms
10 eggs
8 ounces (227 g) shredded cheese

4 ounces (113 g) butter
6 chopped scallions
4 ounces (113 g) leafy greens
1 tsp. salt
1 tsp. ground black pepper
1 tbsp. fresh parsley
1 cup keto-friendly mayonnaise

1. Preheat the oven to 350°F (180°C).
2. Combine the olive oil and vinegar in a bowl. Stir well and set aside.
3. Make the frittata: In a nonstick skillet, melt the butter over medium-high heat. Add the mushrooms and cook until lightly browned. Reserve the melted butter to grease a baking dish.
4. Take a plate, and combine the scallions, fried mushrooms, and parsley. Season with salt and pepper.
5. Combine the eggs, cheese, mayonnaise, salt, and pepper in another bowl. Whisk until well combined.
6. Add the mushroom mixture to the bowl and stir well.
7. Pour the mixture into the greased baking dish. Place the dish into the preheated oven and bake for about 40 minutes.
8. Divide the mixture among four plates. Cool for 5 minutes and then serve with the vinaigrette and leafy greens.

REHEAT: Microwave, covered, until the desired temperature is reached or reheat in a frying pan or air fryer / instant pot, covered, on medium.
SERVE IT WITH: To make this a complete meal, serve with keto vanilla milkshake.
PER SERVING
calories: 1084 | fat: 104.0g | total carbs: 8.0g | fiber: 3.0g | protein: 32.0g

Recipe 2 (Lunch/Dinner): Bacon Salad with Feta Cheese | Fat 81% | Protein 15% | Carbs 4%

Makes: 4 servings **Prep time:** 20 minutes **Store:** In an airtight container in the fridge for up to 4 days or in the freezer for up to 1 month.

5 ounces (142 g) bacon, chopped
5 sun-dried tomatoes in oil, sliced
1 cup feta cheese, crumbled
4 basil leaves

2 tsps. extra-virgin olive oil
1 tsp. balsamic vinegar
Salt, to taste

1. Put the bacon in a saucepan, cook over medium heat for 4 minutes on each side.
2. Transfer the bacon to a paper towel-lined plate, using a slotted spoon to drain excess fat.
3. In a salad bowl, add the tomato slices.
4. Scatter crumbled cheese and basil leaves over the tomatoes, then top with cooked bacon.
5. Drizzle the olive oil and vinegar over the mixture, then sprinkle with salt.
6. Let stand for 5 minutes before serving.

REHEAT: Microwave the bacon, covered, until the desired temperature is reached or reheat the bacon in a frying pan or air fryer / instant pot, covered, on medium.
SERVE IT WITH: To make this a complete meal, you can serve it with grilled chicken thighs or pork chops.
PER SERVING
calories: 272 | fat: 24.7g | total carbs: 2.9g | fiber: 0.2g | protein: 10.0g

Recipe 3 (Lunch/Dinner): Garlicky Mushrooms and Spinach Italian Style | Fat 74% | Protein 12% | Carbs 14%

Makes: 4 servings **Prep time:** 20 minutes **Store:** In an airtight container in fridge for 3 days or freezer for up to 3 months.

14 ounces (397 g) sliced mushrooms
10 ounces (284 g) clean fresh spinach, roughly chopped
½ cup white wine
2 chopped garlic cloves

2 tbsps. olive oil
1 chopped scallion
2 tbsps. balsamic vinegar
Salt and freshly ground black pepper, to taste
Chopped fresh parsley, for garnish

1. Heat the oil in a large skillet over medium-high heat.
2. Sauté the garlic and scallion until tender texture, then add the mushrooms and cook until they shrink.
3. Add the spinach, cook for a few minutes until it wilts.
4. Add the vinegar, stir well.
5. Add the white wine and cook on low until the wine has absorbed.
6. Season with salt and pepper, then stir well.
7. Transfer to a platter, top with a sprinkle of fresh parsley and serve while warm.

REHEAT: Microwave, covered, until the desired temperature is reached or reheat in a frying pan or instant pot, covered, on medium.
SERVE IT WITH: To make this a complete meal, serve the mushroom and spinach with your favorite chicken.

PER SERVING
calories: 172 | fat: 14.1g | total carbs: 8.6g | fiber: 2.7g | protein: 5.3g

Recipe 4 (Lunch/Dinner): Easy Air Fryer Lemon Chicken | Fat 70% | Protein 27% | Carbs 3%

Makes: 4 servings **Prep time:** 10 minutes **Store:** In an airtight container in the fridge for up to 4 days or in the freezer for up to 1 month.

4 skin-on, bone-in chicken thighs
4 lemon wedges
¼ cup lemon juice
2 cloves garlic, minced

1 tsp. Dijon mustard
⅛ tsp. ground black pepper
¼ tsp. salt
2 tbsps. olive oil

1. Combine the lemon juice, garlic, salt, black pepper, olive oil, and mustard together in a bowl.
2. Coat the chicken thighs with the marinade and put them into a Ziploc bag. Seal the bag and put it in the refrigerator for at least 2 hours.
3. Preheat the air fryer to 375°F (190°C).
4. Take out the chicken and dry it with paper towels.
5. Fry the chicken in the air fryer basket in batches for 22 to 24 minutes and a meat thermometer should read 165°F (74°C). Flip the chicken thighs during the cooking.
6. Remove from the air fryer to a plate and squeeze the lemon wedges over. Serve warm.

REHEAT: Microwave, covered, until the desired temperature is reached or reheat in a frying pan or air fryer / instant pot, covered, on medium.
SERVE IT WITH: To make this a complete meal, you can serve it with stir-fried zoodles.

PER SERVING
calories: 503 | fat: 39.0g | total carbs: 5.5g | fiber: 0.3g | protein: 32.3g

Prep Plan #2

Meal Plan	Breakfast	Lunch	Dinner
Day-1	Beef and Vegetable Hash	Keto Cauliflower Bake with Cheese	Easy Beef Brisket
Day-2	(Not Keto)	Baked Chicken and Mushrooms	Keto Cauliflower Bake with Cheese
Day-3	Creamy Bacon Omelet with Onion (Plan #4)	Garlic Portobello Mushrooms	Baked Chicken and Mushrooms
Day-4	(Not Keto)	Easy Beef Brisket	Keto Cauliflower Bake with Cheese
Day-5	Beef and Vegetable Hash	Baked Chicken and Mushrooms	Garlic Portobello Mushrooms
Day-6	Garlic Portobello Mushrooms	Keto Cauliflower Bake with Cheese	Easy Beef Brisket
Day-7	Beef and Vegetable Hash	Easy Beef Brisket	Baked Chicken and Mushrooms

Shopping List

* ½ lb ground beef
* 2 lbs beef brisket
* 2 boneless chicken breasts, skin-on
* Eggs
* Mushrooms
* 2 zucchinis

* Red bell pepper
* Onions
* 1 head cauliflower
* Heavy whipping cream
* Ground nutmeg
* 4 lemon wedges

Beef and Vegetable Hash

Keto Cauliflower Bake with Cheese

Baked Chicken and Mushrooms

Easy Beef Brisket

Recipe 1 (Breakfast): Beef and Vegetable Hash | Fat 64% | Protein 27% | Carbs 9%

Makes: 4 servings **Prep time:** 15 minutes **Store:** Transfer the cooked beef and veggie mixture into a large container and refrigerate for 1 to 2 days.

½ pound (227 g) ground beef
4 eggs
½ of zucchini, chopped
½ of red bell pepper, seeded and chopped
¼ of onion, chopped
1½ cups sugar-free tomato sauce

2 tsps. garlic, minced
1 tbsp. dried basil, crushed
1 tsp. dried oregano, crushed
2 tsps. olive oil
Sea salt and ground black pepper, to taste

1. Heat the oil over medium-high heat in a large deep saucepan. Cook the beef, stirring occasionally, until browned.
2. Add the zucchini, bell pepper, onion and garlic, cook for about 3 minutes, stirring frequently.
3. Add the tomato sauce, dried herbs, salt and black pepper, then bring to a gentle boil. Cook for about 10 minutes, stirring occasionally.
4. Use the back of a spoon to create 4 wells in the beef mixture. Crack an egg into each well. Reduce the heat to medium-low and cook until desired doneness.
5. Serve warm.

SERVE IT WITH: Fresh green salad goes great with this dish.

PER SERVING
calories: 268 | fat: 19.2g | total carbs: 8.0g | fiber: 2.0g | protein: 17.8g

Recipe 2 (Lunch/Dinner): Keto Cauliflower Bake with Cheese | Fat 82% | Protein 13% | Carbs 5%

Makes: 4 servings **Prep time:** 15 minutes **Store:** In an airtight container in the fridge for up to 3 days. It is not recommended to freeze.

1 head cauliflower, cut into florets
1 tsp. mixed herbs
½ tsp. black pepper, ground
1 tsp. salt
3 tbsps. olive oil

1 tbsp. butter
½ cup heavy whipping cream
1 pinch nutmeg, ground
1 cup Cheddar cheese, shredded
3 tbsps. Parmesan cheese, grated

1. Start by preheating the oven to 450°F (235°C) and then line an aluminum foil in a baking sheet.
2. Spread the cauliflower florets over the baking sheet, then sprinkle with mixed herbs, pepper, salt, and olive oil. Toss to coat well.
3. Place the baking sheet into the preheated oven. Bake for 10 to 15 minutes.
4. Put a saucepan over medium heat, then heat the butter, heavy whipping cream, nutmeg and Cheddar cheese. Simmer for 5 minutes and keep stirring during the cooking.
5. Scatter the mixture and Parmesan cheese over the cauliflower, and place back into the oven for 10 minutes
6. Remove from the oven. Let stand for 5 minutes before serving.

REHEAT: Microwave, covered, until the desired temperature is reached or reheat in a frying pan or air fryer / instant pot covered, on medium.
SERVE IT WITH: To make this a complete meal, serve with baked shrimp scampi.

PER SERVING
calories: 329 | fat: 30.1g | total carbs: 5.3g | fiber: 1.6g | protein: 10.7g

Recipe 3 (Lunch/Dinner): Baked Chicken and Mushrooms | Fat 56% | Protein 36% | Carbs 8%

Makes: 4 servings **Prep time:** 10 minutes **Store:** In an airtight container in the fridge for up to 4 days or in the freezer for up to 1 month.

2 boneless chicken breasts, skin-on	½ cup of water
8 ounces (227 g) fresh mushrooms, cut into ¼-inch-thick slices	1 tbsp. butter
	2 tbsps. olive oil
	Salt and ground black pepper, to taste

1. Preheat the oven to 400°F (205°C).
2. Season the chicken with salt and pepper.
3. In a frying pan, heat the olive oil over medium-high heat. Add the chicken breasts, skin side down, and cook for 5 minutes.
4. Flip the chicken, add the mushrooms and salt and cook for 5 minutes, stirring occasionally.
5. Place the chicken in the oven and bake for 15 to 20 minutes.
6. Transfer to a plate. Cover it with a foil and set aside.
7. Put the pan over medium-high heat and cook the mushrooms for 5 minutes. Add the water and scrape up the bits with a wooden spoon. Cook for 2 minutes.
8. Remove from the heat and add any juices from the chicken to the pan. Add the butter and mix until it has melted completely.
9. Sprinkle salt and pepper. Top the chicken with mushroom mixture. Serve.

REHEAT: Microwave, covered, until the desired temperature is reached or reheat in a frying pan or instant pot, covered, on medium.
SERVE IT WITH: To make this a complete meal, serve it on a bed of zucchini noodles.

PER SERVING
calories: 368 | fat: 23.2g | total carbs: 8.5g | fiber: 1.3g | protein: 31.2g

Recipe 4 (Lunch/Dinner): Easy Beef Brisket | Fat 72% | Protein 27% | Carbs 1%

Makes: 4 servings **Prep time:** 5 minutes **Store:** In an airtight container in the refrigerator for up to 4 days or in the freezer for up to 1 month.

2 pounds (907 g) beef brisket	2 minced garlic cloves
1 tbsp. butter	1 small sliced onion
	Salt and freshly ground black pepper, to taste

1. Heat butter in a large nonstick skillet over medium heat, then add garlic and onion.
2. Sauté for 3 minutes and then add black pepper, salt, and beef briskets.
3. Cover and cook for 30 minutes over medium-low heat.
4. Remove from the nonstick skillet and slice into 1-inch (2.5-cm) sizes before serving.

REHEAT: Microwave, covered, until the desired temperature is reached or reheat in a frying pan or air fryer / instant pot, covered, on medium.
SERVE IT WITH: To make this a complete meal, serve with grilled chicken salad.

PER SERVING
calories: 665 | fat: 53.1g | total carbs: 2.4g | fiber: 0.3g | protein: 41.4g

Recipe 5 (Snack): Garlic Portobello Mushrooms | Fat 80% | Protein 3% | Carbs 17%

Makes: 3 servings **Prep time:** 10 minutes **Store:** In an airtight container in the fridge for up to 3 days.

3 portobello mushrooms	4 tbsps. balsamic vinegar
¼ cup olive oil	3 tbsps. onions, chopped
4 garlic cloves, minced	

1. Remove mushroom stems. Reserve them for other use.
2. Place the mushroom caps on a platter, grills facing up.
3. In a small bowl, combine the oil, vinegar, garlic, and onions. Pour the mixture evenly over the mushroom caps. Marinade for about 1 hour.
4. Preheat the grill to medium-high heat.
5. Cook for 10 minutes, flipping them halfway through.
6. Transfer to a plate to cool for about 5 minutes before serving.

REHEAT: Microwave, covered, until it reaches the desired temperature.
SERVE IT WITH: To make this a delicious complete meal, serve the grilled mushrooms with a hearty topping.

PER SERVING
calories: 206 | fat: 18.3g | total carbs: 9.1g | fiber: 1.3g | protein: 2.2g

Prep Plan #3

Meal Plan	Breakfast	Lunch	Dinner
Day-1	Avocado Eggs with Spicy Sauce	Creamy Tarragon Chicken	Baked Salmon Fillets
Day-2	Tomato Cilantro Salsa	Spinach Salad with Dijon Vinaigrette	Creamy Tarragon Chicken
Day-3	Avocado Eggs with Spicy Sauce	Baked Salmon Fillets	Spinach Salad with Dijon Vinaigrette
Day-4	Beef and Vegetable Hash (Plan #2)	Tomato Cilantro Salsa	Baked Salmon Fillets
Day-5	Avocado Eggs with Spicy Sauce	Creamy Tarragon Chicken	Tomato Cilantro Salsa
Day-6	Tomato Cilantro Salsa	Spinach Salad with Dijon Vinaigrette	Creamy Tarragon Chicken
Day-7	Avocado Eggs with Spicy Sauce	Baked Salmon Fillets	Spinach Salad with Dijon Vinaigrette

Shopping List

* 1 lb salmon fillets
* 4 skinless, boneless chicken breasts
* Eggs
* Tomatoes
* White onions
* 1 avocado
* Heavy cream
* Spinach

* Bacon
* Jalapeños
* Tarragon
* Spring onions
* 1 head of lettuce
* Cilantro
* Tomatillo

Creamy Tarragon Chicken

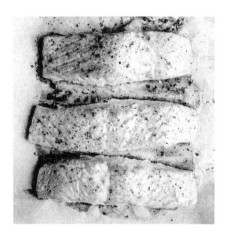

Baked Salmon Fillets

Spinach Salad with Dijon Vinaigrette

Tomato Cilantro Salsa

Recipe 1 (Breakfast): Avocado Eggs with Spicy Sauce | Fat 79% | Protein 12% | Carbs 9%

Makes: 4 servings **Prep time:** 15 minutes **Store:** In an airtight container in the fridge for up to 4 days. It is not recommended to freeze.

8 eggs
2 cups crushed tomatoes
1 white onion, minced
2 fresh jalapeños, minced
2 garlic cloves, minced
½ cup olive oil, divided

Salt and freshly ground black pepper, to taste
sliced avocado, queso fresco, and cilantro for serving

1. Heat ⅓ olive oil in a skillet over medium heat. Add the jalapeños to the pan, and cook until slightly tender. Add the onion and garlic, and stir until the onion is translucent.
2. Add the crushed tomatoes into the pan and turn to low heat. Cook until the sauce has thickened, then season with salt and pepper. Transfer the tomato mixture to a plate.
3. Heat the remaining oil in the skillet over medium heat.
4. Crack the eggs into the frying pan, one at a time. Fry for 2 minutes, then sprinkle with salt and pepper. Add tomato mixture, stir and cook 1 minute more.
5. Divide the egg mixture among four plates. Spread sliced avocado, queso fresco, and cilantro evenly on each plate. Serve whilst still hot.

REHEAT: Microwave the egg mixture, covered, until the desired temperature is reached or reheat in a frying pan or air fryer / instant pot, covered, on medium.
SERVE IT WITH: To make this a complete meal, serve it with a glass of sparkling water.
PER SERVING
calories: 513 | fat: 45.0g | total carbs: 17.0g | fiber: 6.0g | protein: 16.0g

Recipe 2 (Lunch/Dinner): Creamy Tarragon Chicken | Fat 41% | Protein 58% | Carbs 1%

Makes: 4 servings **Prep time:** 15 minutes **Store:** In an airtight container in the fridge for up to 4 days or in the freezer for up to 1 month.

4 skinless, boneless chicken breasts
½ cup heavy cream
1 tbsp. butter
1 tbsp. olive oil

1 tbsp. Dijon mustard
2 tsps. chopped fresh tarragon
Salt and fleshly ground black pepper, to taste

1. In a pan over medium-high heat, melt the butter and then add the olive oil.
2. Season the chicken with salt and pepper. Fry the chicken for 15 minutes in the pan on both sides. Transfer to a plate and set aside.
3. Pour the heavy cream into the pan, then add the mustard and the tarragon and simmer for 5 minutes.
4. Add the chicken into the pan and cover it with creamy sauce.
5. Transfer the chicken to a plate and serve.

REHEAT: Microwave, covered, until the desired temperature is reached or reheat in a frying pan or air fryer / instant pot, covered, on medium.
SERVE IT WITH: To make this a complete meal, serve it with a bowl of green salad.

PER SERVING
calories: 395 | fat: 18.2g | total carbs: 1.2g | fiber: 0.3g | protein: 53.7g

Recipe 3 (Lunch/Dinner): Baked Salmon Fillets | Fat 64% | Protein 32% | Carbs 4%

Makes: 4 servings **Prep time:** 25 minutes **Store:** In an airtight container in the fridge for up to 4 days or in the freezer for up to 1 month.

1 pound (454 g) salmon fillets
¼ cup melted butter
¼ cup lemon juice
1 tbsp. dried dill weed

¼ tsp. garlic powder
Sea salt and fresh ground black pepper, to taste

1. Preheat the oven to 350ºF (180ºC).
2. Arrange the salmon fillets on a lightly greased baking dish.
3. In a bowl, mix the melted butter and lemon juice. Pour the mixture over the fillets. Sprinkle with dill, garlic powder, sea salt, and pepper.
4. Bake the fillets in the preheated oven for 25 minutes.
5. Transfer to a platter and serve while hot.

REHEAT: Microwave, covered, until the desired temperature is reached or reheat in a frying pan or air fryer/instant pot, covered, on medium.
SERVE IT WITH: To make this a complete meal, serve it with sautéed green beans or roasted broccoli.

PER SERVING
calories: 321 | fat: 20.8g | total carbs: 1.6g | fiber: 0.2g | protein: 69.5g

Recipe 4 (Lunch/Dinner): Spinach Salad with Dijon Vinaigrette | Fat 81% | Protein 8% | Carbs 11%

Makes: 4 salads **Prep time:** 15 minutes **Store:** In an airtight container in the fridge for 4 to 5 days.

1 cup spinach
2 bacon slices, chopped
1 spring onion, sliced
½ lettuce head, shredded
1 hard-boiled egg, chopped
1 avocado, sliced

VINAIGRETTE:
1 tsp. Dijon mustard
¼ tsp. garlic powder
1 tbsp. white wine vinegar
3 tbsps. olive oil
Salt, to taste

1. In a nonstick skillet, cook bacon over medium heat for 8 minutes. Transfer to plate lined with a paper towel to drain and cool.
2. Combine spinach, onion, lettuce, and chopped egg in a medium mixing bowl. Stir to combine well.
3. Prepare a separate bowl, add all the vinaigrette ingredients, and whisk together until well mixed.
4. Pour the vinaigrette dressing over the spinach mixture and toss to coat well.
5. Top with cooked bacon and avocado slices. Serve.

REHEAT: Microwave the bacon, if needed, covered, until the desired temperature is reached or reheat the bacon in a frying pan or air fryer / instant pot, covered, on medium.
SERVE IT WITH: To make this a complete meal, serve it with sliced button mushrooms and fried chicken.

PER SERVING
calories: 273 | fat: 25.2g | total carbs: 8.2g | fiber: 4.8g | protein: 6.1g

Recipe 5 (Snack): Tomato Cilantro Salsa | Fat 8% | Protein 11% | Carbs 81%

Makes: 4 servings **Prep time:** 10 minutes **Store:** In an airtight container in the fridge for up to 4 days. It is not recommended to freeze.

4 chopped large tomatoes
½ cup chopped fresh cilantro
3 cloves minced garlic
1 minced jalapeño pepper

1 chopped onion
1 diced tomatillo
1 tbsp. lime juice
Salt, to taste

1. Mix the tomatoes, cilantro, onion, garlic, tomatillo, salt, lime juice and jalapeño pepper in a bowl. Stir well to combine.
2. Cover with plastic wrap. Chill it for about 24 hours. Serve

SERVE IT WITH: To make this a complete meal, serve the dish with zucchini chips.

PER SERVING
calories: 56 | fat: 0.5g | total carbs: 12.3g | fiber: 3.1g | protein: 2.4g

Prep Plan #4

Meal Plan	Breakfast	Lunch	Dinner
Day-1	Creamy Bacon Omelet with Onion	Sauteed Garlic Asparagus	Creamy Mushroom Pork Tenderloin
Day-2	Scrambled Eggs and Tomatoes	Garlic Spinach Soup	Sauteed Garlic Asparagus
Day-3	Creamy Bacon Omelet with Onion	Creamy Mushroom Pork Tenderloin	Garlic Spinach Soup Creamy Vanilla Ice Cream
Day-4	Scrambled Eggs and Tomatoes	Garlic Spinach Soup Creamy Vanilla Ice Cream	Creamy Mushroom Pork Tenderloin
Day-5	Creamy Bacon Omelet with Onion	Sauteed Garlic Asparagus	Baked Chicken and Mushrooms (Plan #2)
Day-6	Scrambled Eggs and Tomatoes	Scrambled Eggs and Tomatoes	Sauteed Garlic Asparagus
Day-7	Creamy Bacon Omelet with Onion	Creamy Mushroom Pork Tenderloin	Garlic Spinach Soup Creamy Vanilla Ice Cream

Shopping List

* Eggs
* 2 lbs pork loin
* 1 lb fresh asparagus spears
* Spinach leaves
* Cheese
* Bacon
* Whipping cream
* Onions
* Canned artichoke hearts

* White mushrooms
* Sour cream
* Chicken stock
* Spring onions
* Tomatoes
* Scallions
* Pickled jalapeños pepper
* Swerve confectioners' style sweetener

Sauteed Garlic Asparagus

Creamy Mushroom Pork Tenderloin

Garlic Spinach Soup

Scrambled Eggs and Tomatoes

Recipe 1 (Breakfast): Creamy Bacon Omelet with Onion | Fat 81% | Protein 15% | Carbs 4%

Makes: 4 servings **Prep time:** 10 minutes **Store:** In an airtight container in the fridge for up to 4 days or in the freezer for up to 1 month.

6 eggs
8 cooked and chopped bacon slices
¼ cup onion, chopped
½ cup canned artichoke hearts, chopped

2 tbsps. heavy whipping cream
1 tbsp. olive oil
Sea salt and ground black pepper, to taste

1. Whisk the eggs in a bowl. Add the bacon and cream, then mix well to combine the ingredients.
2. In a skillet, heat the olive oil over medium-high heat.
3. Sauté the onion for 3 minutes.
4. Make the omelet: Pour the egg mixture into the skillet and tilt pan to evenly distribute across the bottom.
5. Cook the omelet for about 2 minutes. Use a spatula to lift the edges to allow the uncooked egg below spread.
6. Sprinkle the artichoke on the omelet, then flip. Cook for an additional 4 minutes and flip again. Season with salt and pepper.
7. Place onto plates. Serve.

REHEAT: Microwave, covered, until it reaches the desired temperature.
SERVE IT WITH: To make this a complete meal, serve with a light salad.

PER SERVING
calories: 422 | fat: 38.0g | total carbs: 6.0g | fiber: 2.0g | protein: 16.0g

Recipe 2 (Lunch/Dinner): Sauteed Garlic Asparagus | Fat 79% | Protein 13% | Carbs 8%

Makes: 4 servings **Prep time:** 5 minutes **Store:** In an airtight container in the fridge for up to 3 days. It is not recommended to freeze.

1 pound (454 g) fresh asparagus spears, trimmed
¼ cup butter
¼ tsp. ground black

pepper
1 tsp. coarse salt
2 tbsps. olive oil
3 cloves garlic, minced

1. Place the butter in a skillet. Cook over medium-high heat until the butter is melted. Add pepper, salt, and olive oil and garlic. Stir well to combine well cook for 1 minute.
2. Add the asparagus and cook for about 10 minutes. Flip the asparagus halfway through to ensure even cooking.
3. Transfer to a big platter and serve warm.

REHEAT: Microwave, covered, until the desired temperature is reached or reheat in a frying pan or air fryer / instant pot, covered, on medium.
SERVE IT WITH: To make this a complete meal, serve with cooked eggs and shredded Parmesan.

PER SERVING
calories: 85 | fat: 7.4g | total carbs: 5.3g | fiber: 2.5g | protein: 2.7g

Recipe 3 (Lunch/Dinner): Creamy Mushroom Pork Tenderloin | Fat 42% | Protein 53% | Carbs 5%

Makes: 4 servings **Prep time:** 10 minutes **Store:** In an airtight container in the refrigerator for up to 4 days or in the freezer for up to 1 month.

2 pounds (907 g) pork loin
1 cup white mushrooms
¾ cup sour cream

Salt and freshly ground black pepper, to taste
2 tbsps. Butter

1. Put the pork in a bowl, season with black pepper and salt.
2. Heat the butter in a nonstick skillet over medium heat. Add the pork and sauté for 3 minutes.
3. Pour mushroom and sour cream over the pork. Cover and cook for 15 minutes.
4. Remove from heat to serving plates and serve warm.

REHEAT: Microwave, covered, until the desired temperature is reached or reheat in a frying pan or air fryer / instant pot, covered, on medium.
SERVE IT WITH: To make this a complete meal, serve with egg mayo salad.

PER SERVING
calories: 573 | fat: 33.6g | total carbs: 3.8g | fiber: 0.2g | protein: 60.6g

Recipe 4 (Lunch/Dinner): Garlic Spinach Soup | Fat 68% | Protein 15% | Carbs 17%

Makes: 3 servings **Prep time:** 5 minutes **Store:** In an airtight container in the fridge for up to 4 days or in the freezer for up to 1 month.

12 ounces (340 g) spinach leaves	2 garlic cloves
1½ cups chicken stock	1 tbsp. olive oil
½ cup mint leaves	4 tbsps. heavy cream
4 spring onions, chopped	Salt and black pepper, to taste

1. Place a pot over medium heat and heat the oil. Add the onions and garlic. Cook for 3 minutes then add the spinach leaves.
2. Cook for 4 minutes, then add the stock and mint leaves, then pour it into a blender.
3. Pulse until it is smooth, then add the heavy cream, salt, and pepper.
4. Leave the soup in the fridge until ready to serve.

REHEAT: Microwave, covered, until the desired temperature is reached or reheat in a frying pan or instant pot, covered, on medium.
SERVE IT WITH: To make this a complete meal, serve it with some warm keto bread.

PER SERVING
calories: 184 | fat: 13.9g | total carbs: 10.8g | fiber: 3.1g | protein: 7.1g

Recipe 5 (Snack): Scrambled Eggs and Tomatoes | Fat 68% | Protein 24% | Carbs 7%

Makes: 4 servings **Prep time:** 5 minutes **Store:** In an airtight container in the fridge for up to 4 days.

6 eggs	jalapeños pepper
1 ounce (28 g) butter	3 ounces (85 g) shredded cheese
1 chopped tomato	
1 chopped scallion	Salt and freshly ground black pepper, to taste
2 chopped pickled	

1. Melt the butter in a medium pan over medium-high.
2. Add the tomatoes, scallions, and jalapeños, then cook for 4 minutes.
3. In a small bowl, crack the eggs and then add them to the pan. Cook for 2 minutes.
4. Season with the pepper, cheese, and salt. Stir well and serve.

REHEAT: Microwave, covered, until the desired temperature is reached or reheat in a frying pan, covered, on medium.
SERVE IT WITH: To make this a complete meal, serve the eggs with crisp lettuce, avocados, and a dressing to add taste.

PER SERVING
calories: 216 | fat: 16.7g | total carbs: 4.3g | fiber: 0.7g | protein: 12.2g

Recipe 6 (Dessert): Creamy Vanilla Ice Cream | Fat 93% | Protein 2% | Carbs 5%

Makes: 3 servings **Prep time:** 10 minutes **Store:** In an airtight container in your freezer for 1 month.

1 cup heavy whipping cream	1 tsp. vanilla extract
	1 tbsp. vodka
2 tbsps. Swerve confectioners' style sweetener	¼ tsp. xanthan gum
	1 pinch salt

1. In a large jar, add the cream, vodka, xanthan gum, Swerve, vanilla extract, and salt.
2. Use a hand blender to beat the cream mixture until the cream has thickened.
3. Cover and put it in the refrigerator for 3 to 4 hours, stirring occasionally.
4. Take out the vanilla ice cream and serve.

SERVE IT WITH: To make this a complete meal, serve the ice cream with toasted nuts.

PER SERVING
calories: 143 | fat: 14.8g | total carbs: 1.6g | fiber: 0g | protein: 0.8g

Prep Plan #5

Meal Plan	Breakfast	Lunch	Dinner
Day-1	Baked Avocado Eggs	Iceberg Lettuce and Bacon Salad	Low Carb Garlic Chicken
Day-2	Mushroom Cheese Frittata (Plan #1)	Bacon Collard Greens	Iceberg Lettuce and Bacon Salad
Day-3	Baked Avocado Eggs	Low Carb Garlic Chicken	Bacon Collard Greens
Day-4	Mushroom Cheese Frittata (Plan #1)	Iceberg Lettuce and Bacon Salad	Low Carb Garlic Chicken
Day-5	Baked Avocado Eggs	Bacon Collard Greens	Baked Salmon Fillets (Plan #3)
Day-6	Mushroom Cheese Frittata (Plan #1)	Low Carb Garlic Chicken	Iceberg Lettuce and Bacon Salad
Day-7	Baked Avocado Eggs	Baked Salmon Fillets (Plan #3)	Bacon Collard Greens

Shopping List

* 1 Whole chicken
* Eggs
* 2 Avocados
* Chicken breast
* Cheddar cheese
* One 12 oz pack of bacon

* 1 Head iceberg lettuce
* Gorgonzola cheese
* Collard greens
* Cayenne pepper
* Chicken stock
* Romano cheese

Recipe 1 (Breakfast): Baked Avocado Eggs | Fat 71% | Protein 24% | Carbs 5%

Makes: 4 servings **Prep time:** 10 minutes **Store:** In an airtight container in the fridge for up to 4 days or in the freezer for up to 1 month.

2 peeled and pitted avocados, halved lengthwise	shredded
4 eggs	¼ cup Cheddar cheese, shredded
1 (4-ounce / 113-g) cooked chicken breast,	Sea salt and freshly ground black pepper, to taste

1. Preheat the oven to 425°F (220°C).
2. Use a spoon to double the size of the hole in each avocado half and place on a baking dish, hollow parts facing up.
3. Crack an egg into each hole and divide the chicken breast between every half of the avocado. Sprinkle with the Cheddar cheese. Season with salt and pepper.
4. Bake for about 20 minutes.
5. Arrange on four serving plates. Serve whilst still hot.

REHEAT: Microwave, covered, until it reaches the desired temperature.
SERVE IT WITH: To make this a complete meal, serve with strawberry zucchini chia smoothie.

PER SERVING
calories: 330 | fat: 26.0g | total carbs: 8.0g | fiber: 4.0g | protein: 20.0g

Recipe 2 (Lunch): Iceberg Lettuce and Bacon Salad | Fat 78% | Protein 16% | Carbs 6%

Makes: 4 servings **Prep time:** 9 minutes **Store:** In an airtight container in the fridge for 2 days.

4 ounces (113 g) bacon	vinegar
1 head iceberg lettuce, separated into leaves	3 tbsps. extra virgin olive oil
1½ cups Gorgonzola cheese, crumbled	2 tbsps. pumpkin seeds
1 tbsp. white wine	Salt and freshly ground black pepper, to taste

1. Chop the bacon into bite-sized pieces.
2. Cook the bacon in a nonstick skillet over medium heat for 6 minutes.
3. Transfer to plate lined with paper towels to drain the excess fat and cool

4. In a medium-sized mixing bowl, add vinegar, oil, salt, and pepper. Stir thoroughly until the mixture is perfectly combined.
5. Put the lettuce leaves on a platter and top it with cooked bacon and cheese. Pour the vinegar mixture over the salad and toss until well coated.
6. Top with pumpkin seeds, then let stand for 10 minutes before serving.

REHEAT: Microwave the bacon, if needed, covered, until the desired temperature is reached or reheat the bacon in a frying pan or air fryer / instant pot, covered, on medium.
SERVE IT WITH: To make this a complete meal, serve it with green and egg drip soup or veggie skewers.

PER SERVING
calories: 432 | fat: 37.9g | total carbs: 7.6g | fiber: 2.5g | protein: 17.2g

Recipe 3 (Lunch): Bacon Collard Greens | Fat 74% | Protein 20% | Carbs 6%

Makes: 4 servings **Prep time:** 15 minutes **Store:** In an airtight container in the fridge for up to one week.

1 (1½- to 2-pound / 680- to 907-g) bunch collard greens, rinsed and trimmed	Cayenne pepper, to taste
	⅓ cup vinegar
	Salt and freshly ground black pepper, to taste
6 slices bacon	

1. In a large skillet, cook the bacon slices over medium-high heat on each side until browned evenly. Transfer to a plate.
2. Heat a pot of water on low until boiling. Add the cooked bacon, black pepper, collard greens, cayenne pepper, salt, and vinegar. Cook for 30 minutes, stirring occasionally.
3. Remove from heat to a serving bowl. Serve warm.

REHEAT: Microwave, covered, until the desired temperature is reached or reheat in a frying pan or instant pot, covered, on medium.
SERVE IT WITH: To make this a complete meal, serve the tasty collard greens with smoked turkey especially for dinner.

PER SERVING
calories: 199 | fat: 16.4g | total carbs: 9.7g | fiber: 6.9g | protein: 10.1g

Makes: 4 servings **Prep time:** 10 minutes **Store:** In an airtight container in the fridge for up to 4 days or in the freezer for up to 1 month.

1 (2- to 3-pound / 0.9- to 1.4-kg) whole chicken, cut into uniform pieces
1 cup chicken stock
1 clove garlic, crushed
¼ cup grated Romano cheese

3 tbsps. balsamic vinegar
1 tsp. dried oregano
Salt and freshly ground black pepper, to taste
⅛ cup extra virgin olive oil

1. Preheat the oven to 450°F (235°C).
2. Pour the olive oil and chicken stock over the chicken in a baking dish. Sprinkle with the garlic. Season with oregano, salt, and pepper, then scatter the cheese over the chicken.
3. Bake in the preheated oven for 45 to 60 minutes.
4. Transfer the chicken to a plate. Drizzle with the vinegar and serve.

REHEAT: Microwave, covered, until the desired temperature is reached or reheat in a frying pan or air fryer / instant pot, covered, on medium.
SERVE IT WITH: To make this a complete meal, serve it with a bowl of green salad.

PER SERVING
calories: 389 | fat: 17.7g | total carbs: 5.1g | fiber: 0.1g | protein: 52.3g

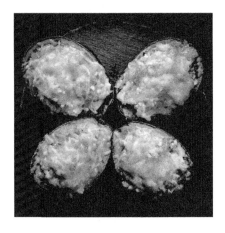

Baked Avocado Eggs

Bacon Collard Greens

Prep Plan #6

Meal Plan	Breakfast	Lunch	Dinner
Day-1	Bacon, Egg, and Cheese Muffins	Sautéed Beef and Brussel Sprouts	Sauteed Garlic Asparagus (Plan #4)
Day-2	Baked Avocado Eggs (Plan #5)	Sour and Spicy Grilled Chicken Breasts	Cheesy Creamed Spinach Casserole
Day-3	Cheese and Ham Omelet	Cheesy Creamed Spinach Casserole	Sour and Spicy Grilled Chicken Breasts
Day-4	Bacon, Egg, and Cheese Muffins	Sour and Spicy Grilled Chicken Breasts	Sauteed Garlic Asparagus (Plan #4)
Day-5	Baked Avocado Eggs (Plan #5)	Cheesy Creamed Spinach Casserole	Sour and Spicy Grilled Chicken Breasts
Day-6	Bacon, Egg, and Cheese Muffins	Sauteed Garlic Asparagus (Plan #4)	Cheesy Creamed Spinach Casserole
Day-7	Cheese and Ham Omelet	Sautéed Beef and Brussel Sprouts	Sauteed Garlic Asparagus (Plan #4)

Shopping List

* Eggs
* ½ lb ground beef
* 4 skinless, boneless chicken breast halves
* Spinach
* 1 package dry onion soup mix
* Brussels sprouts
* 5 oz smoked deli ham
* 1 head of fresh broccoli

* Bacon
* Sriracha hot sauce
* Sour cream
* Paprika
* Green bell peppers
* Yellow onions
* Heavy whipping cream

Bacon, Egg, and Cheese Muffins

Cheesy Creamed Spinach Casserole

Sautéed Beef and Brussel Sprouts

Cheese and Ham Omelet

Recipe 1 (Breakfast): Bacon, Egg, and Cheese Muffins | Fat 66% | Protein 31% | Carbs 3%

Makes: 3 servings **Prep time:** 20 minutes **Store:** In an airtight container in the fridge for up to 4 days or in the freezer for up to 1 month.

1 cup broccoli, chopped
6 beaten eggs
3 slices bacon
A few drops of Sriracha hot sauce
1 cup Cheddar cheese, shredded

½ tsp. black pepper, ground
¼ tsp. garlic powder
½ tsp. salt
SPECIAL EQUIPMENT:
A 6-cup muffin pan

1. Preheat the oven to 350°F (180°C) and line 6 cups of muffin pan with silicone liners.
2. Put the broccoli into a pot of water, cook for 6 to 8 minutes, then chop into ¼-inch pieces.
3. Fry the slices of bacon in a nonstick skillet until crispy, dry them on a paper towel.
4. Take out a bowl, pour in the beaten eggs. Add pepper, garlic, hot sauce, and salt. Stir the mixtures until they are well mixed together.
5. Put the broccoli into the muffin cups. Top with the bacon, Cheddar cheese, and the egg mixture.
6. Bake for 25 minutes.
7. Place onto serving plates. Serve.

REHEAT: Microwave, covered, until it reaches the desired temperature.
SERVE IT WITH: To make this a complete meal, serve with coconut blackberry mint smoothie.

PER SERVING
calories: 296 | fat: 21.6g | total carbs: 6.5g | fiber: 4.0g | protein: 23.0g

Recipe 2 (Lunch/Dinner): Cheesy Creamed Spinach Casserole | Fat 68% | Protein 16% | Carbs 16%

Makes: 4 servings **Prep time:** 10 minutes **Store:** In an airtight container in the fridge for up to 3 days. It is not recommended to freeze.

2 (10-ounce / 284-g) packages frozen chopped spinach, cooked and drained
1 (1-ounce / 28-g) package dry onion soup mix

2 cups sour cream
½ cup Cheddar cheese, shredded
2 tbsps. olive oil, for greasing

1. Preheat the oven to 350°F (180°C) and then spray a casserole dish with olive oil.
2. Take out a medium mixing bowl, add the soup mix, sour cream, and spinach. Stir well to combine. Pour the mixture into the casserole dish and then scatter with the shredded cheese.
3. Place in the preheated oven until cooked through and the cheese melts.
4. Remove from the oven. Cool for 5 minutes before serving.

REHEAT: Microwave, covered, until the desired temperature is reached or reheat in a frying pan or air fryer / instant pot, covered, on medium.
SERVE IT WITH: To make this a complete meal, serve it with the fried fish.

PER SERVING
calories: 339 | fat: 25.6g | total carbs: 18.7g | fiber: 4.9g | protein: 13.3g

Recipe 3 (Lunch/Dinner): Sour and Spicy Grilled Chicken Breasts | Fat 45% | Protein 54% | Carbs 1%

Makes: 4 servings **Prep time:** 10 minutes **Store:** In an airtight container in the fridge for up to 4 days or in the freezer for up to 1 month.

4 skinless, boneless chicken breast halves	⅓ tsp. paprika
1 lemon, juiced	2 tbsps. olive oil, divided
2 tsps. crushed garlic	⅛ cup extra virgin olive oil
1½ tsps. black pepper	1 tsp. salt

1. In a bowl, combine the **extra virgin** olive oil, lemon, garlic, salt, pepper, and paprika. Set aside.
2. Cut 3 slits into the chicken breasts. Take out a separate bowl, add the chicken and pour the marinade over it.
3. Cover with plastic wrap and put in the refrigerator to marinate overnight.
4. Preheat the grill to medium heat and brush the grill grates with 1 tbsp. of olive oil.
5. Take the chicken out from the refrigerator and place it on the grill, cook for about 5 minutes. Flip the chicken over and brush with the remaining 1 tbsp. of olive oil. Cook for another 3 minutes.

REHEAT: Microwave, covered, until the desired temperature is reached or reheat in a frying pan or air fryer / instant pot, covered, on medium.
SERVE IT WITH: To make this a complete meal, serve it with cheesy baked asparagus or creamy cucumber salad.

PER SERVING
calories: 399 | fat: 19.8g | total carbs: 2.1g | fiber: 0.4g | protein: 53.4g

Recipe 4 (Lunch/Dinner): Sautéed Beef and Brussel Sprouts | Fat:78% | Protein 18% | Carbs 4%

Makes: 2 servings **Prep time:** 10 minutes **Store:** In an airtight container in the fridge for up to 4 days or in the freezer for up to 1 month.

5 ounces (142 g) ground beef	Salt and freshly ground black pepper, to taste
4½ ounces (128 g) Brussels sprouts	¼ cup keto-friendly mayonnaise
1½ ounces (43 g) butter	

1. In a large pan over medium heat, melt 3 tbsps. of butter. Add the beef and cook for about 8 minutes.

2. Turn down the heat and add Brussels sprouts, black pepper, salt and the remaining butter. Cooks for 8 more minutes. Stir periodically.
3. Transfer to serving plates. Top with keto-friendly mayonnaise and serve.

REHEAT: Microwave, covered, until the desired temperature is reached or reheat in a frying pan or air fryer / instant pot, covered, on medium.
SERVE IT WITH: To make this a complete meal, serve with broccoli slaw.

PER SERVING
calories: 513 | fat: 44.8g | total carbs: 5.9g | fiber: 2.4g | protein: 22.3g

Recipe 5 (Snack): Cheese and Ham Omelet | Fat 73% | Protein 23% | Carbs 4%

Makes: 2 servings **Prep time:** 5 minutes **Store:** In an airtight container in the fridge for up to 4 days. It is not recommended to freeze.

5 ounces (142 g) diced smoked deli ham	pepper
6 eggs	½ chopped yellow onion
3 ounces (85 g) shredded cheese	2 tbsps. heavy whipping cream or sour cream
2 ounces (57 g) butter	Salt and freshly ground pepper, to taste
½ chopped green bell	

1. In a bowl, whisk the cream and eggs fluffy, then season with pepper and salt. Stir well.
2. Add half of the shredded cheese.
3. Melt the butter in a large pan over medium heat. Add the peppers, ham, and onions and fry for 5 minutes. Add the egg mixture and cook until it is almost firm.
4. Lower the heat, then top with the remaining cheese.
5. Remove from the pan and slice in half before serving.

REHEAT: Microwave, covered, until the desired temperature is reached or reheat in a frying pan, covered, on medium.
SERVE IT WITH: To make this a complete meal, serve the omelet with your preferred green salad. The omelet also goes well with jalapeños and low-carb Sriracha sauce.

PER SERVING
calories: 872 | fat: 71.3g | total carbs: 10.7g | fiber: 0.5g | protein: 46.9g

Prep Plan #7

Meal Plan	Breakfast	Lunch	Dinner
Day-1	Easy Capicola Egg Cups	Spinach Chicken Parmesan	Cheddar Crackers with Garlic
Day-2	Garlic Mushrooms and Bacon	Baked Salmon Steaks with Onion and Dill	Low Carb Garlic Chicken (Plan #5)
Day-3	Easy Capicola Egg Cups	Cheddar Crackers with Garlic	Spinach Chicken Parmesan
Day-4	Garlic Mushrooms and Bacon	Spinach Chicken Parmesan	Baked Salmon Steaks with Onion and Dill
Day-5	Easy Capicola Egg Cups	Baked Salmon Steaks with Onion and Dill	Cheddar Crackers with Garlic
Day-6	Garlic Mushrooms and Bacon	Cheddar Crackers with Garlic	Spinach Chicken Parmesan
Day-7	Garlic Mushrooms and Bacon	Garlic Mushrooms and Bacon	Baked Salmon Steaks with Onion and Dill

Shopping List

* Eggs
* 1½ lbs skinless, boneless chicken breast
* 1 lb salmon fillets
* Capicola
* Heavy cream
* Chicken broth

* Spinach
* Nutritional yeast
* Uncured bacon strips
* Fresh wild mushrooms
* Homemade chicken stock
* Fresh thyme

Easy Capicola Egg Cups

Spinach Chicken Parmesan

Baked Salmon Steaks with Onion and Dill

Cheddar Crackers with Garlic

Recipe 1 (Breakfast): Easy Capicola Egg Cups | Fat 74% | Protein 23% | Carbs 3%

Makes: 3 servings **Prep time:** 5 minutes **Store:** In an airtight container in the fridge for up to 4 days or in the freezer for up to 1 month.

6 slices capicola	1 tbsp. olive oil
6 large eggs	Thinly sliced basil, for
¾ cup Cheddar cheese, shredded	garnish
Salt and freshly ground black pepper, to taste	**SPECIAL EQUIPMENT:** A 6-cup muffin pan

1. Preheat the oven to 400°F (205°C). Spray the muffin cups with olive oil.
2. Place a slice of capicola in each cup, forming a bowl shape.
3. Sprinkle 2 tbsps. of cheese into every cup.
4. Crack an egg into each cup and season with salt and pepper.
5. Bake for about 14 minutes.
6. Serve hot. Garnished with the basil.

REHEAT: Microwave, covered, until it reaches the desired temperature.
SERVE IT WITH: To make this a complete meal, serve with keto green lemon smoothie.

PER SERVING
calories: 307 | fat: 25.3g | total carbs: 2.3g | fiber: 0g | protein: 17.4g

Recipe 2 (Lunch/Dinner): Spinach Chicken Parmesan | Fat 54% | Protein 40% | Carbs 6%

Makes: 4 servings **Prep time:** 10 minutes **Store:** In an airtight container in the fridge for up to 4 days or in the freezer for up to 1 month.

1½ pounds (680 g) skinless, boneless chicken breast, thinly sliced	grated
	1 cup spinach, chopped
	½ cup sun-dried tomatoes, chopped
1 cup heavy cream	1 tsp. garlic powder
½ cup chicken broth	1 tsp. Italian seasoning
½ cup Parmesan cheese,	2 tbsps. olive oil

1. In a large skillet over medium-high heat, heat the olive oil.
2. Add the chicken to the skillet and cook for 3 to 5 minutes on each side. Remove the chicken from the skillet and set aside.
3. Pour the heavy cream into the skillet and add the garlic powder, Italian seasoning, chicken broth, and Parmesan cheese, then whisk well for 5 minutes.
4. Add the spinach and the tomatoes and cook on low heat for 1 minute. Put the chicken back into the skillet and cook for 2 to 3 minutes and keep stirring.
5. Transfer to plates and serve.

REHEAT: Microwave, covered, until the desired temperature is reached or reheat in a frying pan or instant pot, covered, on medium.
SERVE IT WITH: To make this a complete meal, serve it with Greek salad or coleslaw.

PER SERVING
calories: 437 | fat: 26.1g | total carbs: 7.7g | fiber: 1.2g | protein: 44.0g

Recipe 3 (Lunch/Dinner): Baked Salmon Steaks with Onion and Dill | Fat 35% | Protein 64% | Carbs 1%

Makes: 4 servings **Prep time:** 5 minutes **Store:** In an airtight container in the fridge for up to 4 days or in the freezer for up to 1 month.

1 pound (454 g) salmon fillets	½ tsp. ground black pepper
1 tsp. dried dill weed	2 tbsps. melted butter
1 tsp. onion powder	Salt, to taste

1. Preheat the oven to 400ºF (205ºC).
2. Place the salmon fillets on a lightly greased baking dish.
3. Sprinkle with dill, pepper, salt, and onion powder. Rub the butter over the steaks evenly.
4. In the preheated oven, bake the fillets for 20 minutes.
5. Transfer to a platter and serve while hot.

REHEAT: Microwave, covered, until the desired temperature is reached or reheat in a frying pan or air fryer/instant pot, covered, on medium.
SERVE IT WITH: The salmon steaks perfectly go well with crunchy cabbage slaw or grilled zucchini.

PER SERVING
calories: 431 | fat: 16.9g | total carbs: 0.9g | fiber: 0.2g | protein: 69.1g

Recipe 4 (Lunch/Dinner): Cheddar Crackers with Garlic | Fat 67% | Protein 29% | Carbs 4%

Makes: 4 servings **Prep time:** 15 minutes **Store:** Place the crackers in an airtight container and store at room temperature for up to 1 week.

1 cup almond flour
½ cup Cheddar cheese, shredded finely
1 tbsp. nutritional yeast
¼ tsp. baking soda
¼ tsp. garlic powder

¼ tsp. sea salt
2 tsp. olive oil
1 egg
Olive oil spray

1. Preheat the oven to 350°F (180°C) and line a baking sheet with parchment paper. Brush parchment papers with olive oil spray.
2. Combine the almond flour, Cheddar cheese, nutritional yeast, baking soda, garlic powder, and salt in a large mixing bowl, and mix well.
3. Crack an egg in another bowl, and add the oil, beat until well combined. Pour the egg mixture into the flour mixture. Mix well until a dough ball forms.
4. Knead the dough for 1 to 2 minutes with your hands. Transfer the dough ball to the greased parchment paper, then press into a disk. Arrange another greased parchment paper on top of dough, then roll it into a 9×12-inch rectangle with a rolling pin. Cut the edges of the dough into an even rectangle. Now, cut the dough into 1½×1½-inch columns and rows. Bake the crackers for about 15 to 20 minutes.
5. Transfer to a wire rack to cool before serving.

SERVE IT WITH: Spread a thin layer of cream cheese over crackers and top with crispy bacon bits before serving.

PER SERVING
calories: 184 | fat: 13.8g | total carbs: 1.8g | fiber: 0.3g | protein: 7.2g

Recipe 5 (Snack): Garlic Mushrooms and Bacon | Fat 49% | Protein 19% | Carbs 33%

Makes: 4 servings **Prep time:** 15 minutes **Store:** In an airtight container in the fridge for up to 4 days or in the freezer for up to 1 month.

6 uncured bacon strips, chopped
4 cups fresh wild mushrooms, sliced
2 tsps. garlic, minced

2 tbsps. homemade chicken stock
1 tbsp. fresh thyme, chopped

1. Put the bacon in a large nonstick skillet over medium-high heat and cook for about 7 minutes, stirring frequently. Add the mushrooms and garlic and sauté for another 7 minutes. Add the chicken stock and stir to scrape up any browned bits from the bottom of skillet.
2. Transfer to serving plates. Top with fresh thyme and serve warm.

REHEAT: Microwave, covered, until the desired temperature is reached or reheat in a frying pan or air fryer / instant pot, covered, on medium.
SERVE IT WITH: Serve this dish with your favorite greens.
TIP: Topping of Parmesan cheese will enhance the flavor of bacon and mushrooms.

PER SERVING
calories: 67 | fat: 3.9g | total carbs: 6.0g | fiber: 2.6g | protein: 3.9g

Prep Plan #8

Meal Plan	Breakfast	Lunch	Dinner
Day-1	Low Carb Jambalaya with Chicken and Sausage	Simple Baked Cabbage	Skillet Pork Chops with Coconut
Day-2	Mushroom-Spinach Soup	Skillet Pork Chops with Coconut	Brussels Sprouts with Bacon and Vinegar
Day-3	Low Carb Jambalaya with Chicken and Sausage	Brussels Sprouts with Bacon and Vinegar	Simple Baked Cabbage
Day-4	Vanilla Chocolate Mug Cake	Mushroom-Spinach Soup Vanilla Chocolate Mug Cake	Skillet Pork Chops with Coconut
Day-5	Low Carb Jambalaya with Chicken and Sausage	Simple Baked Cabbage	Brussels Sprouts with Bacon and Vinegar
Day-6	Vanilla Chocolate Mug Cake	Skillet Pork Chops with Coconut	Mushroom-Spinach Soup Vanilla Chocolate Mug Cake
Day-7	Low Carb Jambalaya with Chicken and Sausage	Brussels Sprouts with Bacon and Vinegar	Simple Baked Cabbage

Shopping List

* Eggs
* Fresh cabbages
* Brussels sprouts
* One 12 oz pack of bacon
* 1½ lbs thick boneless pork chops
* 4 sausages
* Skinless chicken thighs
* Unsweetened coconut milk
* Unsweetened coconut
* Green onions
* Celery
* Chicken broth

* Cauliflowers
* Tomatoes
* Lard
* Parsley
* Basil
* Ginger
* Spinach
* Mushrooms
* Vegetable stock
* Cayenne pepper
* Sugar-free dark chocolate chips
* Granulated monk fruit sweetener

Simple Baked Cabbage

Skillet Pork Chops with Coconut

Mushroom-Spinach Soup

Brussels Sprouts with Bacon and Vinegar

Recipe 1 (Breakfast): Low Carb Jambalaya with Chicken and Sausage | Fat 76% | Protein 20% | Carbs 4%

Makes: 4 servings Prep time: 25 minutes Store: In an airtight container in the fridge for up to 4 days.

4 (8-ounce / 227-g) cooked and chopped sausage	2 tbsps. Cajun seasoning
	½ cup chicken broth
	2½ cups riced cauliflower
1 cup cubed skinless chicken thighs, cooked	¼ cup diced tomatoes
	⅓ cup lard
½ cup green onions, chopped	Handful of freshly chopped parsley
1¼ cups diced celery	

1. Place the lard in a frying pan. Cook until the lard is melted and then add the sausage, chicken thighs, green onions, celery, and Cajun seasoning. Cook for about 10 minutes, stirring occasionally.
2. Add the chicken broth and riced cauliflower. Cover and cook for about 5 minutes.
3. Add the diced tomatoes and stir. Increase the heat and cook uncovered until the liquid has evaporated.
4. Transfer to four bowls to cool for 5 minutes before serving. Top with the parsley.

REHEAT: Microwave, covered, until it reaches the desired temperature.
SERVE IT WITH: To make this a complete meal, serve with slow-cooked mushroom and chicken soup.

PER SERVING
calories: 446 | fat: 37.7g | total carbs: 7.6g | fiber: 3.4g | protein: 22.5g

Recipe 2 (Lunch/Dinner): Simple Baked Cabbage | Fat 88% | Protein 4% | Carb 8%

Makes: 4 servings Prep time: 10 minutes Store: In an airtight container in the fridge for up to 4 days or in the freezer for up to 1 month.

2 pounds (907 g) fresh cabbage, cored and sliced into wedges	melted
	¼ tsp. ground black pepper
6 ounces (170 g) butter,	1 tsp. salt

1. Preheat the oven to 400°F (205°C).
2. Place the wedges on the baking sheet in the oven without overlapping.
3. Sprinkle the ground pepper and salt on the wedges for seasoning, and pour the melted butter over it.
4. Put the cabbage in the baking sheet and bake for about 20 minutes.
5. Remove from the oven and serve warm.

REHEAT: The dish can reheat and use it as a fresh salad. Microwave it as per the instruction or reheat in a frying pan or air fryer or instant pot under moderate heat.
SERVE IT WITH: Serve it as a side dish along with roasted meat, chicken, or fish. Sprinkle spices of your choice for unique taste other than ground pepper.

PER SERVING
calories: 366 | fat: 35.3g | total carbs: 8.0g | fiber: 6.0g | protein: 3.0g

Recipe 3 (Lunch/Dinner): Skillet Pork Chops with Coconut | Fat 71% | Protein 26% | Carbs 3%

Makes: 4 servings Prep time: 10 minutes Store: In an airtight container in the fridge for up to 4 days or in the freezer for up to 1 month.

1½ pounds (680 g) ¾-inch thick boneless pork chops	divided
	2 tbsps. fresh lime juice
1 cup unsweetened coconut milk	1 tsp. fresh basil, chopped
½ cup unsweetened coconut, shredded	1 tbsp. fresh ginger, grated
¼ cup coconut oil,	2 tbsps. garlic, minced

1. In a large nonstick skillet over medium heat, melt 2 tbsps. of coconut oil. Add the pork chops and cook until browned on both sides, flipping occasionally. Transfer to a plate. Set aside.
2. Add the remaining coconut oil and sauté the ginger and garlic for about 2 minutes. Put the pork chops back into the skillet, add the coconut milk, lime juice and basil and stir to combine. Cover and simmer for about 12 to 15 minutes.
3. Transfer to serving plates. Garnish with shredded coconut and serve.

REHEAT: Microwave, covered, until the desired temperature is reached or reheat in a frying pan or air fryer / instant pot, covered, on medium.
SERVE IT WITH: Enjoy these pork chops with fresh green salad.

PER SERVING
calories: 491 | fat: 39.0g | total carbs: 6.1g | fiber: 3.0g | protein: 32.0g

Recipe 4 (Lunch/Dinner): Mushroom-Spinach Soup | Fat 83% | Protein 6% | Carbs 11%

Makes: 3 servings **Prep time:** 10 minutes **Store:** In an airtight container in the fridge for up to 4 days or in the freezer for up to 1 month.

1 cup spinach, torn into small pieces	chopped
½ cup mushrooms, chopped	½ tsp. tamari
	1 tsp. sesame seeds, roasted
3 cups vegetable stock	Salt and freshly ground
1 tbsp. olive oil	black pepper, to taste
1 tsp. garlic, finely	

1. Heat the olive oil in a saucepan over medium heat.
2. Add garlic and sauté for 30 seconds.
3. Add spinach and mushrooms, then sauté for 1 minute.
4. Add salt, black pepper, tamari, and vegetable stock. Cook for another 3 minutes. Stir constantly.
5. Serve with the garnishing of sesame seeds.

REHEAT: Microwave, covered, until the desired temperature is reached or reheat in a slow cooker or instant pot, covered, on medium.
SERVE IT WITH: To make this a complete meal, serve the spinach mushrooms soup with roasted asparagus sticks on the side.

PER SERVING
calories: 80 | fat: 7.4g | total carbs: 3.2g | fiber: 1.1g | protein: 1.2g

Recipe 5 (Lunch/Dinner): Brussels Sprouts with Bacon and Vinegar | Fat 71% | Protein 16% | Carbs 13%

Makes: 4 servings **Prep time:** 10 minutes **Store:** In an airtight container in the refrigerator for up to 4 days.

1¼ pounds (567 g) Brussels sprouts, cut into strips	1 lemon, juiced
	1 tbsp. olive oil
	3 tbsps. erythritol
4 ounces (113 g) sliced bacon	Salt and freshly ground black pepper, to taste
⅓ cup apple cider vinegar	Cayenne pepper, to taste

1. Heat the olive oil in a nonstick skillet over medium heat. Add bacon and cook for 8 minutes, flipping occasionally.
2. Add the erythritol, apple cider vinegar, and lemon

juice, black pepper, salt and cayenne pepper. Stir to combine well. Lower the heat and cook for 1 minute more.
3. Arrange the bacon mixture in a large bowl and add the Brussels sprouts. Gently toss until well combined.
4. Let stand for 5 minutes before serving.

SERVE IT WITH: To make this a complete meal, serve with beef steak and berry smoothie.

PER SERVING
calories: 248 | fat: 15.0g | total carbs: 13.9g | fiber: 5.4g | protein: 8.4g

Recipe 6 (Dessert): Vanilla Chocolate Mug Cake | Fat 77% | Protein 16% | Carbs 7%

Makes: 4 servings **Prep time:** 5 minutes **Store:** In an airtight container in the fridge or covered at room temperature for 1 day.

2 beaten eggs	1 tbsp. granulated monk fruit sweetener
¼ cup melted butter	
½ cup sugar-free dark chocolate chips	1¼ tsps. baking powder
	½ tsp. vanilla extract
½ cup almond flour	2 tbsps. coconut flour
2 tbsps. cocoa powder	

1. In a medium mixing bowl, combine the coconut flour, almond flour, cocoa powder, monk fruit sweetener and baking powder, stir well to combine.
2. Add eggs, vanilla extract, and butter to the mixture, stir well to combine.
3. Add the chocolate chips, stir until well distributed in the batter.
4. Separate the mixture into two mugs. Microwave for 1½ minutes.
5. Cool for 10 minutes and serve.

SERVE IT WITH: To make this a complete meal, serve it with a dollop of plain Greek yogurt.

PER SERVING
calories: 470 | fat: 40.0g | total carbs: 9.3g | fiber: 1.1g | protein: 19.4g

Prep Plan #9

Meal Plan	Breakfast	Lunch	Dinner
Day-1	Sausage Egg and Cheese Breakfast Casserole	Mayonnaise Egg Salad	Pressure Cooker Beef Roast
Day-2	Baked Avocado Eggs (Plan #5)	Baked Cheesy Zucchini	Mayonnaise Egg Salad
Day-3	Sausage Egg and Cheese Breakfast Casserole	Pressure Cooker Beef Roast	Baked Cheesy Zucchini
Day-4	Baked Avocado Eggs (Plan #5)	Mayonnaise Egg Salad	Pressure Cooker Beef Roast
Day-5	Sausage Egg and Cheese Breakfast Casserole	Baked Cheesy Zucchini	Low Carb Garlic Chicken (Plan #5)
Day-6	Baked Avocado Eggs (Plan #5)	Pressure Cooker Beef Roast	Baked Cheesy Zucchini
Day-7	Sausage Egg and Cheese Breakfast Casserole	Low Carb Garlic Chicken (Plan #5)	Mayonnaise Egg Salad

Shopping List

* 2 lb beef
* 1 lb bulk breakfast sausage
* Cream cheese
* Eggs
* Yellow onions

* Heavy whipping cream
* Green onions
* 2 zucchinis
* Sour cream
* Beef broth

Recipe 1 (Breakfast): Sausage Egg and Cheese Breakfast Casserole | Fat 81% | Protein 17% | Carbs 2%

Makes: 4 servings **Prep time:** 15 minutes **Store:** In an airtight container in the fridge for up to 4 days or in the freezer for up to 1 month.

1 pound (454 g) bulk breakfast sausage	1 cup Cheddar cheese, shredded
6 whisked eggs	⅓ cup heavy whipping cream
2 tbsps. coconut oil	
1 tbsp. butter, unsalted	½ tsp. ground black pepper
⅓ cup yellow onions, chopped	
1 pressed clove garlic	1 tsp. salt

1. Preheat the oven to 350°F (180°C) and spray a baking dish with coconut oil.
2. Place the butter in a skillet. Cook until the butter is melted. Add the onions, sauté for about 4 minutes.
3. Add the sausage, cook until browned evenly. Drain excess butter and set aside.
4. Take out a bowl, add the whisked eggs, garlic, cream, pepper, and salt, whisk until well combined.
5. Spread the sausage evenly over the baking dish, then top with cheese. Add the egg mixture.
6. Bake for about 35 minutes.
7. Place onto plates, cool for about 5 minutes before serving.

REHEAT: Microwave, covered, until it reaches the desired temperature.
SERVE IT WITH: To make this a complete meal, serve it with a cup of unsweetened coconut milk.

PER SERVING
calories: 977 | fat: 88.2g | total carbs: 5.0g | fiber: 0.2g | protein: 41.1g

Recipe 2 (Lunch/Dinner): Mayonnaise Egg Salad | Fat 80% | Protein 18% | Carbs 2%

Makes: 4 servings **Prep time:** 6 minutes **Store:** In an airtight container in the refrigerator for up to 4 days

8 eggs	3 cups water
¼ cup green onion, chopped	1 tsp. yellow mustard
	¼ tsp. paprika
½ cup keto-friendly mayonnaise	Salt and freshly ground black pepper, to taste

1. Heat water and eggs in a saucepan until boiling.
2. Leave the eggs in the hot water for 12 minutes.
3. Arrange the eggs in a bowl of cold water. Peel and chop the eggs into chunks.
4. Prepare another bowl, add the chopped eggs, mustard, green onion and mayonnaise, and toss to combine well.
5. Season with the paprika, pepper and salt and stir well. Serve.

SERVE IT WITH: To make this a complete meal, serve it between gluten-free almond bread or coconut crackers.

PER SERVING
calories: 449 | fat: 39.9g | total carbs: 2.9g | fiber: 0.3g | protein: 18.4g

Recipe 3 (Lunch/Dinner): Baked Cheesy Zucchini | Fat 80% | Protein 10% | Carb 10%

Makes: 4 servings **Prep time:** 5 minutes **Store:** In an airtight container in the fridge for up to 4 days or in the freezer for up to 1 month.

1 (8-ounce / 227-g) package softened cream cheese	¼ cup shredded Parmesan cheese
1 large zucchini	1 tbsp. finely chopped garlic
1 cup sour cream	Ground paprika, to taste

1. Preheat the oven to 350°F (180°C).
2. Bring a pot of water to a boil. Add the zucchini and cook for 15 minutes. Cut the zucchini into half and into lengthwise, and then scoop out the seeds.
3. Combine the garlic, sour cream, Parmesan cheese, and cream cheese in a medium bowl. Pour the mixture into zucchini halves and sprinkle the paprika on top.
4. Place the stuffed zucchini in a lightly greased baking pan. Bake in the oven for 10 to 15 minutes.
5. Remove from the oven and serve hot.

REHEAT IT: Microwave, covered, until the desired temperature is reached or reheat in a frying pan or instant pot, covered, on medium.
SERVE IT WITH: To make this a complete meal, serve it with baked or roasted chicken.

PER SERVING
calories: 313 | fat: 27.8g | total carbs: 8.3g | fiber: 0.2g | protein: 7.5g

Recipe 4 (Lunch/Dinner): Pressure Cooker Beef Roast | Fat 41% | Protein 57% | Carbs 2%

Makes: 4 servings **Prep time:** 10 minutes **Store:** In an airtight container in the fridge for up to 4 days or in the freezer for up to 1 month.

2 pounds (907 g) beef roast
1 cup onion soup

1 cup beef broth
Salt and freshly ground black pepper, to taste

1. In a pressure cooker, add beef roast, onion soup, beef broth, black pepper and salt. Put the lid on and cook for 50 minutes at high pressure.
2. Let the pressure naturally release. Transfer to a serving plate to cool before serving.

REHEAT: Microwave, covered, until the desired temperature is reached or reheat in a frying pan or air fryer / instant pot, covered, on medium.
SERVE IT WITH: To make this a complete meal, serve with creamy cucumber salad.

PER SERVING
calories: 432 | fat: 19.2g | total carbs: 2.7g | fiber: 0.5g | protein: 61.8g

Sausage Egg and Cheese Breakfast Casserole

Mayonnaise Egg Salad

Baked Cheesy Zucchini

Pressure Cooker Beef Roast

Prep Plan #10

Meal Plan	Breakfast	Lunch	Dinner
Day-1	Paleo Egg Muffins	Keto Coleslaw	Juicy Grilled Chicken Breast
Day-2	Shaved Brussels Sprouts Salad	Juicy Grilled Chicken Breast	Thai-Style Pork
Day-3	Paleo Egg Muffins	Thai-Style Pork	Keto Coleslaw
Day-4	Shaved Brussels Sprouts Salad	Shaved Brussels Sprouts Salad	Juicy Grilled Chicken Breast
Day-5	Paleo Egg Muffins	Keto Coleslaw	Brussels Sprouts with Bacon and Vinegar (Plan #8)
Day-6	Shaved Brussels Sprouts Salad	Juicy Grilled Chicken Breast	Thai-Style Pork
Day-7	Paleo Egg Muffins	Thai-Style Pork	Keto Coleslaw

Shopping List

* Eggs
* 4 skinless, boneless chicken breast halves
* Brussels sprouts
* 8 oz cooked ham
* 1 lb thinly sliced pork loin
* Cabbages

* Red bell peppers
* Onions
* Liquid stevia
* Chicken stock
* Cilantro

Paleo Egg Muffins

Keto Coleslaw

Juicy Grilled Chicken Breast

Thai-Style Pork

Recipe 1 (Breakfast): Paleo Egg Muffins | Fat 61% | Protein 31% | Carbs 8%

Makes: 4 servings **Prep time:** 15 minutes **Store:** In an airtight container for 1 to 2 days or keep in the fridge for up to 1 week.

8 ounces (227 g) cooked ham, crumbled	pepper
8 eggs	¼ tsp. salt
1 cup red bell pepper, diced	2 tbsps. Water
1 cup onion, diced	**SPECIAL EQUIPMENT:** An 8-cup muffin pan, greased with olive oil
⅛ tsp. ground black	

1. Preheat the oven to 350°F (180°C).
2. In a large bowl, whisk together the eggs, ham, red bell pepper, onion, salt, ground black pepper, and water.
3. Fill muffin cups with blend of ingredients, then place the cups in the preheated oven.
4. Bake for 18 minutes.
5. Remove from the oven. Allow to cool for 5 minutes before serving.

REHEAT: Microwave, covered, until the desired temperature is reached or reheat in a frying pan or air fryer / instant pot, covered, on medium.
SERVE IT WITH: To make this a complete meal, serve it with a dollop of plain Greek yogurt or other drinks you like.

PER SERVING
calories: 357 | fat: 24.3g | total carbs: 8.3g | fiber: 1.7g | protein: 27.9g

Recipe 2 (Lunch/Dinner): Keto Coleslaw | Fat 92% | Protein 2% | Carb 6%

Makes: 4 servings **Prep time:** 5 minutes **Store:** Refrigerate the coleslaw in a tight container for later use. It can ideally use for 3 to 4 days if stored well.

8 ounces (227 g) fresh cabbage, cored	⅛ tsp. ground black pepper
½ lemon juice extract	1 tbsp. Dijon mustard
½ cup keto-friendly mayonnaise	⅛ tsp. fennel seeds
	1 tsp. salt

1. Using a food processor, shred the cabbage and place in a medium bowl. Drizzle with the lemon juice, and sprinkle salt and pepper over it.

2. Stir well. Let it sit for about 10 minutes. Drain out excess liquid.
3. Add the mayonnaise and mustard, and stir well to combine.
4. Sprinkle with fennel seeds and serve.

SERVE IT WITH: It is an ideal choice if served along with BBQ, roasted / baked chicken, meat, or fish.

PER SERVING
calories: 209 | fat: 21.7g | total carbs: 3.1g | fiber: 2.4g | protein: 1.3g

Recipe 3 (Lunch/Dinner): Juicy Grilled Chicken Breast | Fat 34% | Protein 65% | Carbs 1%

Makes: 4 servings **Prep time:** 15 minutes **Store:** In an airtight container in the fridge for up to 1 week.

4 skinless, boneless chicken breast halves	2 tbsps. keto-friendly mayonnaise
⅓ cup Dijon mustard	⅓ tbsp. liquid stevia
1 tsp. steak sauce	1 tbsp. olive oil

1. Preheat the grill on medium heat and brush the grill grate with olive oil.
2. In a bowl, combine the steak sauce, mayonnaise, stevia, and mustard. Reserve some mustard sauce for basting in another bowl, then coat the chicken with the remaining sauce.
3. Grill the chicken for about 20 minutes, flipping occasionally and basting frequently with the reserved sauce.
4. Transfer to a plate and serve warm.

REHEAT: Microwave, covered, until the desired temperature is reached or reheat in a frying pan or air fryer / instant pot, covered, on medium.
SERVE IT WITH: To make this a complete meal, serve the grilled chicken with creamy spinach dill.

PER SERVING
calories: 333 | fat: 12.6g | total carbs: 1.5g | fiber: 0.9g | protein: 54.3g

Recipe 4 (Lunch/Dinner): Thai-Style Pork | Fat 55% | Protein 43% | Carbs 2%

Makes: 4 servings **Prep time:** 15 minutes **Store:** In a sealed airtight container in the fridge for up to 3 days or in your freezer for about 1 month.

1 pound (454 g) thinly sliced pork loin
1 cup chicken stock
1 cup dry white wine
1 tbsp. extra-virgin olive oil

1 tbsp. unsalted butter
3 tbsps. fresh cilantro, chopped
Salt and freshly ground black pepper, to taste

1. In a bowl, mix sliced pork salt and black pepper. Set aside.
2. In a large skillet, melt olive oil and butter over medium heat.
3. Put the pork slices in the skillet and cook until browned on both sides.
4. Pour in chicken stock and cook until it thickens, stirring frequently.
5. Reduce the heat, add dry white wine and cook until the liquid is reduced to half.
6. Remove from the heat to serving plates. Serve with the garnishing of cilantro

REHEAT: Microwave, covered, until the desired temperature is reached or reheat in a frying pan or air fryer / instant pot, covered, on medium.
SERVE IT WITH: To add more flavors to this meal, serve the pork loin with zucchini fries. It also tastes great paired with Brussels sprout salad.

PER SERVING
calories: 336 | fat: 18.0g | total carbs: 1.5g | fiber: 0g | protein: 29.6g

Recipe 5 (Lunch/Dinner): Shaved Brussels Sprouts Salad | Fat 84% | Protein 9% | Carbs 7%

Makes: 4 servings **Prep time:** 12 minutes **Store:** In an airtight container in the refrigerator for up to 4 days.

2 ounces (57 g) almonds
1 ounce (28 g) pumpkin seeds
1 ounce (28 g) sunflower seeds
1 tbsp. coconut oil
1 tsp. chili paste
½ tsp. fennel seeds
1 pinch salt

SALAD:
1 pound (454 g) Brussels sprouts, shredded
1 lemon, juice and zest
½ cup spicy almond and seed mix
½ cup olive oil
Salt and freshly ground black pepper, to taste

1. Heat the oil in a frying pan. Add chili, almond, pumpkin seeds, fennel seeds, and sunflower seeds and stir to mix.
2. Add salt and sauté for 2 minutes.
3. Make the salad: Shred the Brussels sprouts in a food processor, then Transfer to a bowl.
4. Prepare another bowl, add the lemon juice and zest, olive oil, pepper and salt, stir well to combine. Pour the mixture over the Brussels sprouts. Toss to combine well and put it in the refrigerator for about 10 minutes.
5. Transfer the salad to a serving plate, add the almond and seeds mixture and stir to combine. Serve.

SERVE IT WITH: To make this a complete meal, serve with roasted salmon.

PER SERVING
calories: 484 | fat: 44.9g | total carbs: 16.8g | fiber: 7.9g | protein: 11.1g

Prep Plan #11

Meal Plan	Breakfast	Lunch	Dinner
Day-1	Cheese Omelet	Garlic Butter Chicken	Arugula, Walnuts and Zucchini Salad
Day-2	Lemon Smoked Salmon Fat Bombs	Keto Seafood Chowder	Garlic Butter Chicken
Day-3	Cheese Omelet	Arugula, Walnuts and Zucchini Salad	Keto Seafood Chowder
Day-4	Lemon Smoked Salmon Fat Bombs	Garlic Butter Chicken	Cheese Omelet
Day-5	Cheese Omelet	Keto Seafood Chowder	Arugula, Walnuts and Zucchini Salad Lemon Smoked Salmon Fat Bombs
Day-6	Lemon Smoked Salmon Fat Bombs	Cheese Omelet	Garlic Butter Chicken
Day-7	Cheese Omelet	Arugula, Walnuts and Zucchini Salad	Keto Seafood Chowder

Shopping List

* 2 lbs chicken drumsticks
* 2 oz Smoked salmon
* Eggs
* 1 lb salmon fillets
* 8 oz shrimps
* Baby spinach
* Celery stalks
* Arugula lettuces
* 1 head Romaine lettuce

* 1 can unsweetened coconut milk
* Sour cream
* Green onions
* Parsley
* Clam juice
* Heavy whipping cream
* Fresh sage
* 2 zucchinis
* Fresh chives

Cheese Omelet

Keto Seafood Chowder

Garlic Butter Chicken

Arugula, Walnuts and Zucchini Salad

Recipe 1 (Breakfast): Cheese Omelet | Fat 73% | Protein 22% | Carbs 5%

Makes: 6 servings **Prep time:** 10 minutes **Store:** Keep in the fridge for up to 3 to 4 days, or wrap in plastic and keep in the fridge for up to 4 weeks.

9 eggs	½ cup sour cream
½ cup unsweetened coconut milk	2 green onions, chopped
¼ cup Cheddar cheese, shredded	1 tsp. butter, melted
	1 tsp. salt

1. Preheat the oven to 350ºF (180ºC).
2. In a bowl, combine the eggs, coconut milk, sour cream, salt and green onions.
3. Brush a baking pan with the melted butter and tilt the pan to make sure the butter covers the bottom evenly. Add the egg mixture.
4. Bake in the preheated oven for 25 minutes. Scatter with the cheese and continue baking for an additional 2 minutes.
5. Transfer to serving plates and serve warm.

REHEAT: Microwave, covered, until the desired temperature is reached or reheat in a frying pan or air fryer / instant pot, covered, on medium.
SERVE IT WITH: To make this a complete meal, serve it with something crispy such as avocado sticks.
PER SERVING
calories: 287 | fat: 23.1g | total carbs: 4.3g | fiber: 0.5g | protein: 15.9g

Recipe 2 (Lunch/Dinner): Garlic Butter Chicken | Fat 66% | Protein 31% | Carbs 3%

Makes: 4 servings **Prep time:** 15 minutes **Store:** Low-carb garlic chicken can be stored covered in the fridge for 1 up to 4 days, it can even be kept in the freezer for 15 days.

2 pounds (907 g) chicken drumsticks	1 lemon, the juice
2 ounces (57 g) butter	7 garlic cloves, sliced
½ cup fresh parsley, finely chopped	Salt and freshly ground black pepper, to taste
	2 tbsps.olive oil

1. Preheat the oven to 450°F (235°C).
2. Grease the baking pan with butter and put the chicken drumsticks. Season the chicken with salt, pepper, olive oil, and lemon juice generously.
3. Sprinkle the garlic and parsley on top.
4. Bake the chicken for 30 to 40 minutes.

5. Remove from the oven. Let stand for a few minutes before serving.

REHEAT: Microwave, covered, until the desired temperature is reached or reheat in a frying pan or air fryer / instant pot, covered, on medium.
SERVE IT WITH: This wonderful recipe is served cold or hot, can be Serve with aioli and a hearty salad and toast with garlic. Some people favor it with a delectable cauliflower mash.
PER SERVING
calories: 542 | fat: 40.0g | total carbs: 4.0g | fiber: 1.0g | protein: 42.0g

Recipe 3 (Lunch/Dinner): Keto Seafood Chowder | Fat 66% | Protein 26% | Carbs 8%

Makes: 4 servings **Prep time:** 20 minutes **Store:** The rest of the mixture can be kept in an airtight container in the fridge for 4 days, and it can also be kept in the freezer for 10 days.

1 pound (454 g) salmon fillets, cut into 1-inch pieces	1 cup clam juice
8 ounces (227 g) shrimp, peeled and deveined	1½ cups heavy whipping cream
2 ounces (57 g) baby spinach	2 tsps. dried sage or dried thyme
5 ounces (142 g) celery stalks, sliced	½ lemon, juiced and zested
4 ounces (113 g) cream cheese	4 tbsps. butter
2 garlic cloves, minced	Salt and freshly ground black pepper, to taste
	Fresh sage, for garnish

1. In a large pot, melt the butter over medium heat. Add celery and garlic. Cook for about 5 minutes, stirring occasionally. Add clam juice, cream, cream cheese, sage, lemon juice and lemon zest. Simmer for about 10 minutes.
2. Add the salmon and shrimp. Simmer until salmon is opaque. Add the baby spinach and stir until wilted. Season with salt and pepper.
3. Serve with the Garnishing of fresh sage.

REHEAT: Microwave, covered, until the desired temperature is reached or reheat in a frying pan or instant pot, covered, on medium.
SERVE IT WITH: You can serve this recipe with keto sesame salmon and cucumber and fennel salad.
PER SERVING
calories: 622 | fat: 46.7g | total carbs: 12.5g | fiber: 1.6g | protein: 38.8g

Recipe 4 (Lunch/Dinner): Arugula, Walnuts and Zucchini Salad | Fat 87% | Protein 4% | Carbs 9%

Makes: 4 servings **Prep time:** 15 minutes **Store:** Store in an airtight container in the refrigerator for up to 5 days.

DRESSING:
1 finely minced garlic clove
¾ cup keto-friendly mayonnaise
2 tsps. lemon juice
2 tbsps. olive oil
¼ tsp. chili powder
½ tsp. salt

SALAD:
4 ounces (113 g) arugula lettuce
3½ ounces (99 g) toasted walnuts, chopped
1 head Romaine lettuce
2 zucchinis, deseeded and cut into ½-inch pieces
¼ cup fresh chives, finely chopped
Salt and freshly ground black pepper, to taste
1 tbsp. olive oil

1. Make the dressing: Mix lemon juice, olive oil, garlic, mayonnaise, chili powder and salt in a bowl. Whisk to combine.
2. Make the salad: Mix arugula, Romaine, and chives in a large bowl. Set aside.
3. Heat the olive oil in a frying pan over medium heat. Add zucchinis, pepper and salt and sauté for 5 minutes.
4. Arrange the zucchinis in the salad bowl, then add the toasted walnuts and pour over the dressing. Gently toss until fully combined. Serve.

SERVE IT WITH: To make this a complete meal, serve with grilled beef or shrimp skewers.

PER SERVING
calories: 587 | fat: 58.2g | total carbs: 13.9g | fiber: 6.7g | protein: 8.2g

Recipe 5 (Snack): Lemon Smoked Salmon Fat Bombs | Fat 90% | Protein 10% | Carbs 0%

Makes: 4 servings **Prep time:** 15 minutes **Store:** In an airtight container in the fridge for up to 4 days or in the freezer for up to 1 month

2 ounces (57 g) smoked salmon
½ cup goat cheese, at room temperature
½ cup butter, at room temperature

2 tsps. freshly squeezed lemon juice
Freshly ground black pepper, to taste

1. Line a baking sheet with parchment paper.
2. Make the fat bombs: Add cheese, lemon juice, smoked salmon, pepper, and butter to a bowl, then stir well to combine.
3. Scoop 1 tbsp. of the butter mixture onto the baking sheet until you make 12 equally sized mounds.
4. Place the sheet in the refrigerator for about 3 hours.
5. Take out the sheet and set it at room temperature for a few minutes before serving.

SERVE IT WITH: To make this a complete meal, you can serve it with plain Greek yogurt.

PER SERVING
calories: 88 | fat: 9.0g | total carbs: 0g | fiber: 0g | protein: 1.9g

Prep Plan #12

Meal Plan	Breakfast	Lunch	Dinner
Day-1	Keto Cheesy Bacon and Egg Cups	Keto Collard Greens	Grilled Pork Kabobs
Day-2	Crispy Bacon & Kale with Fried Eggs	Cream of Zucchini Soup	Juicy Grilled Chicken Breast (Plan #10)
Day-3	Keto Cheesy Bacon and Egg Cups	Grilled Pork Kabobs	Keto Collard Greens
Day-4	Blueberry Chia Pudding with Almond Milk	Keto Collard Greens	Cream of Zucchini Soup
Day-5	Keto Cheesy Bacon and Egg Cups	Cream of Zucchini Soup	Grilled Pork Kabobs
Day-6	Crispy Bacon & Kale with Fried Eggs	Grilled Pork Kabobs	Cream of Zucchini Soup
Day-7	Blueberry Chia Pudding with Almond Milk	Juicy Grilled Chicken Breast (Plan #10)	Keto Collard Greens

Shopping List

* 1 lb pork tenderloin
* Chicken broth
* Eggs
* One 12 oz pack of bacon
* Collard greens
* Kale
* Fresh basil
* Red onions

* Coconut aminos
* Green bell peppers
* Refined avocado oil
* 2 medium zucchinis
* Sour cream
* 1 can unsweetened vanilla almond milk
* 4 to 6 fresh blueberries
* Stevia

Keto Cheesy Bacon and Egg Cups

Crispy Bacon & Kale with Fried Eggs

Grilled Pork Kabobs

Cream of Zucchini Soup

Recipe 1 (Breakfast): Keto Cheesy Bacon and Egg Cups | Fat 58% | Protein 39% | Carbs 3%

Makes: 3 servings **Prep time:** 5 minutes **Store:** In an airtight container in the fridge for up to 4 days or in the freezer for up to 1 month.

6 large eggs	for garnish
3 ounces (85 g) bacon, in slices	Salt and freshly ground black pepper, to taste
3 ounces (85 g) Cheddar cheese, shredded	**SPECIAL EQUIPMENT:** A 6-cup muffin tin, lightly greased with coconut oil
Thinly sliced fresh basil,	

1. Preheat the oven to 400°F (205°C).
2. Arrange a bacon slice in each muffin cup, then add 2 tbsps. of cheese into every cup.
3. Crack an egg into each cup and season with salt and pepper.
4. Bake in the oven for 12 to 14 minutes.
5. Garnish with basil and serve warm.

REHEAT: Microwave, covered, until the desired temperature is reached or reheat in an air fryer or instant pot, covered, on medium.
SERVE IT WITH: To make this a complete meal, serve it with a cup of black tea.

PER SERVING
calories: 154 | fat: 10.0g | total carbs: 1.0g | fiber: 0g | protein: 15.0g

Recipe 2 (Breakfast): Crispy Bacon & Kale with Fried Eggs | Fat 68% | Protein 22% | Carbs 10%

Makes: 2 servings **Prep time:** 5 minutes **Store:** In an airtight container in the fridge for up to 4 days. It is not recommended to freeze.

2 eggs	¾ pound (340 g) kale, chopped
4 ounces (113 g) bacon, chopped into bite-sized pieces	Salt and freshly ground black pepper, to taste

1. In a large frying pan, cook the bacon over medium heat for 4 minutes on each side. Transfer to a bowl.
2. Add the kale to the pan and season with salt and pepper, and then cook for 2 minutes. Transfer to two plates.
3. Break the eggs straight into the pan and cook for 2 minutes. Sprinkle with salt and pepper.
4. Transfer for to serving plates. Top with bacon and fried egg, then serve.

STORAGE: Store in an airtight container in the fridge for up to 4 days. It is not recommended to freeze.
REHEAT: Microwave, covered, until the desired temperature is reached or reheat in a frying pan or air fryer / instant pot, covered, on medium.
SERVE IT WITH: To make this a complete meal, serve it with a glass of sparkling water.

PER SERVING
calories: 355 | fat: 27.0g | total carbs: 14.0g | fiber: 5.0g | protein: 19.0g

Recipe 3 (Lunch/Dinner): Keto Collard Greens | Fat 81% | Protein 10% | Carbs 9%

Makes: 4 servings **Prep time:** 15 minutes **Store:** In an airtight container in the fridge for no more than 3 days.

2 bunches collard greens (18 ounces / 510 g), stems removed, roughly chopped	seasoning
	¼ green bell pepper, sliced thin
½ red onion, sliced thin	¼ cup refined avocado oil
2 tbsps. coconut aminos	Finely ground gray sea salt, to taste
1 tsp. apple cider vinegar	
1 tbsp. Shichimi	

1. Put a frying pan over medium heat, then heat the avocado oil. Add the sliced red onion and cook over medium-low heat until golden brown.
2. Add the collards, vinegar, Shichimi seasoning, and coconut aminos. Cover and cook for another 5 minutes, then top with the bell pepper and gray sea salt.
3. Divide the cooked collards among four bowls and sever warm.

REHEAT: Microwave, covered, until the desired temperature is reached or reheat in a frying pan or instant pot, covered, on medium.
SERVE IT WITH: To make this dish complete, you can top the collards with sesame seeds and serve it with roasted chicken thighs.

PER SERVING
calories: 160 | fat: 14.4g | total carbs: 8.8g | fiber: 5.2g | protein: 3.9g

Recipe 4 (Lunch/Dinner): Grilled Pork Kabobs | Fat 58% | Protein 38% | Carbs 4%

Makes: 4 servings **Prep time:** 15 minutes **Store:** In an airtight container in the fridge for up to 4 days or in the freezer for up to 1 month.

1 (1-pound / 454-g) pork tenderloin, trimmed and cut into 1½-inch pieces	1 tsp. dried basil, crushed
	¼ cup olive oil
1 tbsp. garlic, minced	Sea salt and ground black pepper, to taste
1 tsp. dried parsley, crushed	Olive oil cooking spray
2 tsps. dried oregano, crushed	**SPECIAL EQUIPMENT:** 4 metal skewers

1. Add the oil, garlic, dried herbs, salt, and black pepper to a mixing bowl, stir well to combine. Add the pork pieces and coat with the marinade generously. Cover the bowl with plastic wrap and refrigerate for 2 to 4 hours.
2. Preheat your grill to medium-high heat and grease the grill grate with olive oil spray.
3. Take out the pork pieces and thread onto 4 metal skewers. Place the pork skewers onto the heated grill and cook for about 12 minutes, flipping occasionally.
4. Transfer to a platter to cook for about 5 minutes before serving.

REHEAT: Remove the skewers from the freezer and immediately grill, covered, over medium-high heat for about 15 minutes, flipping frequently.
SERVE IT WITH: Serve these pork kabobs over the bed of torn lettuce.

PER SERVING
calories: 261 | fat: 16.7g | total carbs: 2.2g | fiber: 1.0g | protein: 25.0g

Recipe 5 (Lunch/Dinner): Cream of Zucchini Soup | Fat 43% | Protein 51% | Carbs 6%

Makes: 4 servings **Prep time:** 15 minutes **Store:** In an airtight container in the fridge for up to 2 days or in the freezer for up to 1 month

2 pounds (907 g) chicken broth	into large chunks
	½ small onion, quartered
1 cup Parmesan cheese, freshly grated	Salt and black pepper, to taste
2 garlic cloves	2 tbsps. butter
2 medium zucchinis, cut	4 tbsps. sour cream

1. Prepare a medium pot, add butter, chicken broth, garlic, zucchini, and onion. Cook over medium heat.
2. Heat the mixture until boiling, then lower the heat. Simmer the soup for 20 minutes.
3. Let cool for 10 minutes.
4. Purée the soup with an immersion blender until smooth.
5. Add sour cream, salt, cheese and black pepper, and stir well. Serve whilst still hot.

REHEAT: Microwave, covered, until the desired temperature is reached or reheat in a saucepan or slow cooker / instant pot, covered, on medium.
SERVE IT WITH: To make this a complete meal, serve the zucchini soup with sautéed zucchini noodles on the side.

PER SERVING
calories: 425 | fat: 20.2g | total carbs: 7.0g | fiber: 0.5g | protein: 54.3g

Recipe 6 (Dessert): Blueberry Chia Pudding with Almond Milk | Fat 73% | Protein 17% | Carbs 10%

Makes: 2 servings **Prep time:** 10 minutes **Store:** in a glass container with an airtight cover, or cover it with plastic wrap. The pudding can last up to 5 days in the refrigerator after preparation.

1 cup unsweetened vanilla almond milk	4 to 6 fresh blueberries
	1½ tbsps. stevia
¼ cup chia seeds	

1. Blend the milk and stevia in a blender for 1 minute.
2. Pour the chia seeds in a glass and add the mixture.
3. Make the pudding: Combine the mixture well and then cover the glass with plastic wrap and put it in the refrigerator for 6 to 8 hours. Transfer the pudding into a glass. Top with blueberries and serve.

SERVE IT WITH: The pudding can be used to layer in parfaits, trifles, or as a pie filling, or you can just enjoy it as a lovely dessert.

PER SERVING
calories: 125 | fat: 10.2g | total carbs: 12.9g | fiber: 9.8g | protein: 5.2g

Prep Plan #13

Meal Plan	Breakfast	Lunch	Dinner
Day-1	Keto Cinnamon Cereal	Calamari Salad with Tomatoes and Parsley	Smoked Salmon, Avocado & Egg Butter Bowl
Day-2	Easy Capicola Egg Cups (Plan #7)	Low-carb Asparagus with Walnuts	Calamari Salad with Tomatoes and Parsley
Day-3	Keto Cinnamon Cereal	Smoked Salmon, Avocado & Egg Butter Bowl	Low-carb Asparagus with Walnuts
Day-4	Easy Capicola Egg Cups (Plan #7)	Calamari Salad with Tomatoes and Parsley	Smoked Salmon, Avocado & Egg Butter Bowl
Day-5	Keto Cinnamon Cereal	Juicy Grilled Chicken Breast (Plan #10)	Low-carb Asparagus with Walnuts
Day-6	Easy Capicola Egg Cups (Plan #7)	Low-carb Asparagus with Walnuts	Calamari Salad with Tomatoes and Parsley
Day-7	Keto Cinnamon Cereal	Smoked Salmon, Avocado & Egg Butter Bowl	Juicy Grilled Chicken Breast (Plan #10)

Shopping List

* 4 oz smoked salmon
* 2 avocados
* Eggs
* Golden flaxmeal
* 2 cans unsweetened almond milk
* 12 oz uncooked calamari rings
* Asparagus

* Kalamata olives
* Grape halved tomatoes
* Fresh parsley
* Green onions
* One lemon
* Lemon zest
* Parsley

Recipe 1 (Breakfast): Keto Cinnamon Cereal | Fat 85% | Protein 11% | Carbs 4%

Makes: 6 servings **Prep time:** 15 minutes **Store:** In an airtight container in the fridge for up to 4 days or in the freezer for up to 1 month.

1 cup almond flour
1 tbsp. golden flaxmeal
1 tsp. ground cinnamon
2 tbsps. sunflower seeds
1 tsp. vanilla extract
¼ tsp. salt

2 tbsps. water
1 tbsp. coconut oil
TO SERVE:
6 cups unsweetened almond milk

1. Preheat the oven to 350°F (180°C).
2. Blend golden flaxmeal, cinnamon, flour, sunflower seeds, vanilla extract, and salt in a food processor until the mixture is smooth.
3. Add the water and the coconut oil and pulse until a dough is formed.
4. Place the dough on a parchment paper, then press until it is flat. Cover with another parchment paper and roll the dough until it is 1.5 to 3 mm thick.
5. Cut the dough into 1-inch squares with a knife.
6. Bake for 10 to 15 minutes.
7. Remove from the heat and let stand for 5 minutes before serving. Serve with unsweetened almond milk.

REHEAT: Microwave, covered, until the desired temperature is reached or reheat in an air fryer or instant pot, covered, on medium.
SERVE IT WITH: To make this a complete meal, serve it with a glass of sparkling water.

PER SERVING
calories: 181 | fat: 17.0g | total carbs: 2.0g | fiber: 0g | protein: 5.0g

Recipe 2 (Lunch/Dinner): Calamari Salad with Tomatoes and Parsley | Fat 54% | Protein 43% | Carbs 3%

Makes: 4 servings **Prep time:** 10 minutes **Store:** In an airtight container in the fridge for up to 3 days.

SALAD:
12 ounces (340 g) uncooked calamari rings
½ cup kalamata olives, pitted and halved
1½ cups grape halved tomatoes

½ packed cup fresh parsley, chopped
¼ cup sliced green onions
DRESSING:
½ cup extra-virgin olive oil

2 small minced garlic cloves
½ juiced lemon
½ grated lemon zest

1 tbsp. red wine vinegar
¼ tsp. black pepper
¼ tsp. gray sea salt

1. Steam the calamari in a steamer for 7 minutes, then chill in the fridge for 2 minutes.
2. In a small bowl, combine all the dressing ingredients, then stir to combine well.
3. Place the calamari in a large bowl along with the grape tomatoes, olives, parsley, and green onions. Pour the dressing over it and toss to coat well.
4. Separate the salad into 4 serving bowls and serve.

SERVE IT WITH: To make this a complete meal, you can serve it with rich clam chowder.

PER SERVING
calories: 508 | fat: 30g | total carbs: 4.4g | fiber: 1.3g | protein: 55.1g

Recipe 3 (Lunch/Dinner): Low-carb Asparagus with Walnuts | Fat 81% | Protein 9% | Carbs 10%

Makes: 4 servings **Prep time:** 10 minutes **Store:** In an airtight container in the fridge for at least days or in the freezer for up to two weeks

12 ounces (340 g) asparagus, woody ends trimmed
¼ cup chopped walnuts

1½ tbsps. olive oil
Sea salt and freshly ground pepper, to taste

1. Put a nonstick skillet over medium-high heat, then heat the olive oil.
2. Add the asparagus and cook until soft, then season with salt, and ground black pepper.
3. Add the walnuts, turn the heat off, and stir well to combine.
4. Transfer to platter and serve warm.

REHEAT: Microwave, covered, until the desired temperature is reached or reheat in a frying pan or instant pot, covered, on medium.
SERVE IT WITH: You can top the asparagus with blue cheese on the last minute of cooking time and cook until the cheese melts. It would increase the flavor of the asparagus.

PER SERVING
calories: 126 | fat: 12.2g | total carbs: 4.0g | fiber: 2.1g | protein: 1.3g

Recipe 4 (Lunch/Dinner): Smoked Salmon, Avocado & Egg Butter Bowl | Fat 84% | Protein 11% | Carbs 5%

Makes: 4 servings **Prep time:** 5 minutes **Store:** In an airtight container in the fridge for up to 2 days.

5 ounces (142 g) butter, at room temperature
4 ounces (113 g) smoked salmon
2 avocados
4 eggs

½ tsp. sea salt
¼ tsp. ground black pepper
1 tbsp. fresh parsley, chopped finely
2 tbsps. olive oil

1. In a pot of water, add the eggs and heat on the stove until boiling.
2. Reduce the heat and simmer for 6 to 9 minutes. Transfer to a bowl with cold water.
3. Peel the eggs and cut them finely. Mix the eggs and butter with a fork. Season with pepper and salt.
4. Sprinkle with slices of smoked salmon, finely chopped parsley, and a side of diced avocado tossed in olive oil. Serve.

REHEAT: Place it in the microwave until it reaches the desired temperature.
SERVE IT WITH: To make this a complete meal, serve with cauliflower rice and a green salad.

PER SERVING
calories: 638 | fat: 61.1g | total carbs: 9.8g | fiber: 6.8g | protein: 16.5g

Keto Cinnamon Cereal

Calamari Salad with Tomatoes and Parsley

Low-carb Asparagus with Walnuts

Smoked Salmon, Avocado & Egg Butter Bowl

Prep Plan #14

Meal Plan	Breakfast	Lunch	Dinner
Day-1	Everything Onion Egg Bagel	Air Fryer Vegetables	Arugula Salad with Steak and Tomatoes
Day-2	Keto Cheesy Bacon and Egg Cups (Plan #12)	Baked Salmon with Parmesan Spinach	Air Fryer Vegetables
Day-3	Everything Onion Egg Bagel	Arugula Salad with Steak and Tomatoes	Baked Salmon with Parmesan Spinach
Day-4	Keto Cheesy Bacon and Egg Cups (Plan #12)	Air Fryer Vegetables	Grilled Pork Kabobs (Plan #12)
Day-5	Keto Coffee Smoothie	Baked Salmon with Parmesan Spinach	Arugula Salad with Steak and Tomatoes
Day-6	Keto Cheesy Bacon and Egg Cups (Plan #12)	Grilled Pork Kabobs (Plan #12)	Baked Salmon with Parmesan Spinach
Day-7	Keto Coffee Smoothie	Arugula Salad with Steak and Tomatoes	Air Fryer Vegetables

Shopping List

* 1½ lbs salmon
* 4 sirloin steaks
* Fresh spinach
* Eggs
* Onion flakes
* Unsweetened strong-brewed coffee
* Unsweetened almond milk
* Unsweetened coconut milk
* Mushrooms
* Artichoke hearts

* Asparagus
* One head of broccoli
* Cherry tomatoes
* Fresh parsley
* Sour cream
* Cherry tomatoes
* Arugula
* Green salad
* Flaxseed meal
* Granulated monk fruit sweetener

Keto Coffee Smoothie

Arugula Salad with Steak and Tomatoes

Baked Salmon with Parmesan Spinach

Air Fryer Vegetables

Recipe 1 (Breakfast): Everything Onion Egg Bagel | Fat 67% | Protein 26% | Carbs 7%

Makes: 2 servings **Prep time:** 10 minutes **Store:** In the sealed jar in the fridge for up to six months.

4 eggs
3 tbsps. white sesame seeds
1 tbsp. black sesame seeds

2 tsps. poppy seeds
1 tbsp. onion flakes
1 tsp. garlic flakes
1 tsp. coarse sea salt

1. Heat the eggs in a medium saucepan of water over medium-high heat until boiling. Boil for about 1 minute. Remove from the heat and cover for about 10 minutes. Drain the eggs and transfer to a bowl of cold water.
2. Mix the remaining ingredients in a bowl.
3. Peel and slice the eggs, then transfer them to serving plates. Season with some seasoning mixture and serve.

SERVE IT WITH: Serve these eggs with avocado slices on the side.

PER SERVING
calories: 230 | fat: 17.2g | total carbs: 6.0g | fiber: 2.0g | protein: 14.9g

Recipe 2 (Breakfast): Keto Coffee Smoothie | Fat 92% | Protein 6% | Carbs 2%

Makes: 2 servings **Prep time:** 5 minutes **Store:** Store brewed coffee in ice cube trays and freeze for 1 to 2 weeks.

2 cups unsweetened strong-brewed coffee, frozen in cubes
1 cup unsweetened almond milk
1 cup unsweetened coconut milk

2 tbsps. coconut oil
2 tbsps. chia seeds
2 tbsps. flaxseed meal
1 to 2 tbsps. granulated monk fruit sweetener
⅛ tsp. ground cinnamon

1. In a high-power blender, blend all ingredients until creamy and smooth.
2. Divide the smoothie between two glasses and serve.

SERVE IT WITH: Serve this smoothie with the topping of heavy cream.

PER SERVING

calories: 430 | fat: 44.2g | total carbs: 6.6g | fiber: 4.5g | protein: 6.0g

Recipe 3 (Lunch/Dinner): Air Fryer Vegetables | Fat 74% | Protein 7% | Carbs 19%

Makes: 4 servings **Prep time:** 10 minutes **Store:** In an airtight container in the fridge for no more than 3 days.

1 cup mushrooms, sliced
1 cup artichoke hearts, chopped
1 bunch asparagus, sliced into 3-inch pieces
1 cup broccoli, cut into florets
1 cup cherry tomatoes, halved
½ tsp. sea salt

VINAIGRETTE:
¼ cup fresh parsley, chopped
3 tbsps. white wine vinegar
1 tsp. ground oregano
6 tbsps. extra-virgin olive oil
½ tsp. sea salt

1. Preheat the air fryer to 400ºF (205ºC).
2. Heat the coconut oil in a nonstick skillet over medium heat. Add the shallot and garlic, and sauté for 2 minutes.
3. Add the mushrooms and sauté for another 3 minutes. Add the artichokes, asparagus, and broccoli and sauté for 3 minutes more, stirring occasionally.
4. Place the cooked vegetables in the air fryer basket. Add the cherry tomatoes and salt. Cook for at least 5 minutes.
5. Meanwhile, make the vinaigrette: In a bowl, combine the oregano, parsley, vinegar, olive oil, and salt.
6. Transfer to a plate. Top with the vinaigrette and serve while warm.

REHEAT: Microwave the vegetables, covered, until the desired temperature is reached or reheat in a frying pan or air fryer/instant pot, covered, on medium.
SERVE IT WITH: To make this dish complete, you can serve it with roasted salmon fillets.

PER SERVING
calories: 195 | fat: 16.1g | total carbs: 13.6g | fiber: 4.4g | protein: 3.4g

Recipe 4 (Lunch/Dinner): Baked Salmon with Parmesan Spinach | Fat 55% | Protein 38% | Carbs 7%

Makes: 4 servings **Prep time:** 5 minutes **Store:** This Recipe is freezer friendly, so it can be stored in the freezer for up to 3 months. To freeze, cover each quiche slice tightly in aluminum foil and freeze for up to 3 months.

1½ pounds (680 g) salmon, in pieces
1 pound (454 g) fresh spinach
1 ounce (28 g) Parmesan cheese, grated finely
1 tbsp. chili paste

½ cup sour cream
¼ cup olive oil
Salt and freshly ground black pepper, to taste

1. Preheat oven to 400°F (205°C).
2. Arrange the salmon in a greased baking dish, season with pepper and salt, skin-side down.
3. In a bowl, combine Parmesan cheese, chili paste and sour cream. Pour the mixture over the salmon fillets.
4. Bake in the preheated oven for 20 minutes.
5. In a nonstick skillet, heat the remaining olive oil. Sauté the spinach until it's wilted, and season with pepper and salt.
6. Serve with the oven-baked salmon immediately.

REHEAT: Place it in the microwave until the desired temperature, or reheat in a frying pan.
SERVE IT WITH: To make this a complete meal, serve with riced cauliflower and a green salad.

PER SERVING
calories: 461 | fat: 28.5g | total carbs: 8.0g | fiber: 2.8g | protein: 42.6g

Recipe 5 (Lunch/Dinner): Arugula Salad with Steak and Tomatoes | Fat 42% | Protein 25% | Carbs 33%

Makes: 4 servings **Prep time:** 15 minutes **Store:** In separate airtight containers in the fridge for up to 3 days.

4 sirloin steaks, trimmed
2 cups cherry tomatoes
1 bunch arugula

4 cups green salad
3 tbsps. extra virgin olive oil, divided
2 tbsps. freshly cracked black pepper

1. Coat the steaks with 2 tbsps. olive oil. Put the black pepper on a plate, then press the steaks into the pepper until coated evenly.
2. Preheat the grill to medium-high heat, then grill the steaks for about 5 minutes per side. Transfer to a bowl and keep aside.
3. Brush the tomatoes with remaining oil, then grill for 5 minutes, turning occasionally.
4. Separate the arugula into four serving plates and top with grilled steaks and tomatoes. Serve with green salad.

REHEAT: Microwave the steak, covered, until the desired temperature is reached.

PER SERVING
calories: 238 | fat: 11.2g | total carbs: 10.8g | fiber: 8.2g | protein: 14.9g

Meal Plan	Breakfast	Lunch	Dinner
Day-1	Almond Milk Porridge	Crispy Taco Wings	Salmon Avocado Salad
Day-2	Bacon, Egg, and Cheese Muffins (Plan #6)	Keto Grilled Fish with Kale Pesto	Crispy Taco Wings
Day-3	Almond Milk Porridge	Salmon Avocado Salad	Keto Grilled Fish with Kale Pesto
Day-4	Chocolate-Covered Strawberries	Crispy Taco Wings	Sautéed Beef and Brussel Sprouts (Plan #6)
Day-5	Bacon, Egg, and Cheese Muffins (Plan #6)	Sautéed Beef and Brussel Sprouts (Plan #6)	Salmon Avocado Salad
Day-6	Chocolate-Covered Strawberries	Keto Grilled Fish with Kale Pesto	Crispy Taco Wings
Day-7	Bacon, Egg, and Cheese Muffins (Plan #6)	Salmon Avocado Salad	Keto Grilled Fish with Kale Pesto

Shopping List

* 3 lbs chicken wings
* 6 oz cooked salmon
* 1½ lbs white fish
* Kale
* Eggs
* Zucchinis
* Unsweetened almond milk
* Avocado mayonnaise
* Celery stalks

* Yellow onions
* Flaxseeds
* Erythritol
* 4 raw Brazil nuts
* Fresh berries
* Fresh dill
* Sugar-free dark chocolate chips
* 10 medium-sized fresh strawberries

Almond Milk Porridge

Crispy Taco Wings

Keto Grilled Fish with Kale Pesto

Salmon Avocado Salad

Recipe 1 (Breakfast): Almond Milk Porridge | Fat 82% | Protein 16% | Carbs 2%

Makes: 2 servings **Prep time:** 2 minutes **Store:** In an airtight container in the fridge for up to 4 days or in the freezer for up to 1 month.

PORRIDGE:
1 cup unsweetened almond milk
¼ cup almond meal
½ cup hemp seeds, hulled
1 tbsp. chia seeds
2 tbsps. flaxseeds, roughly ground
1 tbsp. erythritol

¾ tsp. vanilla extract
¾ tsp. ground cinnamon
2 tbsps. coconut oil
TOPPINGS:
4 raw Brazil nuts, roughly chopped
Fresh berries, optional
2 tbsps. hemp seeds, hulled

1. Combine the milk, hemp seeds, chia seeds, flaxseeds, coconut oil, erythritol, vanilla, and cinnamon in a saucepan and stir well. Heat over medium-high heat until boiling.
2. Cover and cook for about 2 minutes.
3. Remove from the heat, then add almond meal and stir. Separate the mixture into 2 bowls. Top with the Brazil nuts, hemp seeds, and berries. Serve immediately.

REHEAT: Microwave, covered, until it reaches the desired temperature.
SERVE IT WITH: To make this a complete meal, serve with low-carb strawberry smoothie.

PER SERVING
calories: 610 | fat: 55.6g | total carbs: 15.2g | fiber: 12.4g | protein: 24.6g

Recipe 2 (Lunch/Dinner): Crispy Taco Wings | Fat 28% | Protein 71% | Carbs 1%

Makes: 5 servings **Prep time:** 5 minutes **Store:** In an airtight container in the fridge for up to 4 days or in the freezer for up to 1 month.

3 pounds (1.4 kg) chicken wings
1 tbsp. taco seasoning mix

2 tsps. olive oil

1. In a Ziploc bag, add the chicken wings, taco seasoning and olive oil.
2. Seal the bag and shake until the chicken is evenly coated.
3. Preheat the air fryer to 350°F (180°C).
4. Add the chicken and cook for 6 minutes on each side.
5. Transfer to a plate and serve.

REHEAT: Microwave, covered, until the desired temperature is reached or reheat in a frying pan or air fryer / instant pot, covered, on medium.
SERVE IT WITH: To make this a complete meal, serve it with a bowl of cauliflower rice and a glass of sparkling water.

PER SERVING
calories: 364 | fat: 11.4g | total carbs: 1.0g | fiber: 0.2g | protein: 59.9g

Recipe 3 (Lunch/Dinner): Keto Grilled Fish with Kale Pesto | Fat 52% | Protein 39% | Carbs 9%

Makes: 4 servings **Prep time:** 10 minutes **Store:** We can store the leftovers in an airtight container in the freezer for up to 4 days. Pesto can be stored in the refrigerator for 3 to 4 days or in the freezer for up to 1 month.

KALE PESTO:
3 ounces (85 g) kale, chopped
2 ounces (57 g) walnuts, shelled
1 garlic clove
3 tbsps. lemon juice
½ tsp. salt
¼ tsp. ground black pepper
2 tsps. olive oil

FISH AND ZUCCHINI:
1½ pounds (680 g) white fish (such as cod), thawed at room temperature, if frozen
2 zucchinis, rinsed and drained, cut into slices
1 tsp. lemon juice
Salt and freshly ground black pepper, to taste
2 tbsps. olive oil, divided

1. Make the kale pesto: Blend the kale, garlic, lemon juice, and walnuts in the food processor, then season with salt and pepper, and then add the olive oil and blend until the mixture becomes creamy.
2. Rub 1 tbsp. of olive oil, salt, pepper, and lemon juice over the zucchini slices.
3. Spray a nonstick skillet with remaining olive oil, and heat over medium-high heat.
4. Put the fish in the skillet and cook for 3 minutes on each side. Season with salt and black pepper. Serve with zucchini and kale pesto.

REHEAT: Reheat the leftovers in the oven until warmed thoroughly.
SERVE IT WITH: To enjoy the meal, serve this dish with cauliflower rice and tangy cucumber salad.

PER SERVING
calories: 321 | fat: 19.5g | total carbs: 8.1g | fiber: 2.8g | protein: 30.3g

Recipe 4 (Lunch/Dinner): Salmon Avocado Salad | Fat 64% | Protein 32% | Carbs 4%

Makes: 4 servings **Prep time:** 3 hours **Store:** In an airtight container in the fridge for up to 3 days.

6 ounces (170 g) cooked salmon, chopped
4 hard-boiled eggs,
peeled and cubed
¾ cup avocado mayonnaise
2 celery stalks, chopped
½ yellow onion, chopped
1 tbsp. chopped fresh dill
Salt and freshly ground black pepper, to taste

1. Mix the avocado mayonnaise, boiled eggs, cooked salmon, celery stalks, dill, yellow onion, salt, and black pepper in a mixing bowl. Stir to combine well.
2. Cover the bowl with plastic wrap and put it in the refrigerator for 3 hours.
3. Serve chilled.

SERVE IT WITH: To make this a complete meal, serve it with fresh vegetables like cherry tomatoes or cucumbers.

PER SERVING
calories: 263 | fat: 18.7g | total carbs: 5.4g | fiber: 2.6g | protein: 20.8g

Recipe 5 (Dessert): Chocolate-Covered Strawberries | Fat 86% | Protein 1% | Carbs 13%

Makes: 2 servings **Prep time:** 5 minutes **Store:** In an airtight container in the fridge for no more than 2 days.

¼ cup sugar-free dark chocolate chips
10 medium-sized fresh
strawberries, rinsed and drained
1½ tsps. coconut oil

1. In a small microwave-safe bowl, melt the chocolate chips and microwave for 1 minute.
2. Add chocolate chips into the bowl and mix until it completely dissolves.
3. Add the oil and mix thoroughly.
4. Line the parchment paper on a baking sheet. Dip ⅔ of each strawberry inside the melted chocolate and set it on the parchment paper.
5. Put the baking sheet in a fridge for 15 minutes.
6. Take out the chocolate from the fridge and serve.

SERVE IT WITH: To make this a complete meal, you can enjoy them as dessert with your low-carb beverage or dry wines.

PER SERVING
calories: 133 | fat 12.6g | total carbs 5.6g | fiber: 1.2g | protein 0.4g

Prep Plan #16

Meal Plan	Breakfast	Lunch	Dinner
Day-1	Almond Milk and Avocado Smoothie	Cheesy Zucchini Manicotti	Creamy Chicken Soup Orange Walnut Bark
Day-2	Orange Walnut Bark	Easy Creamy Pork Tenderloin	Cheesy Zucchini Manicotti
Day-3	Almond Milk and Avocado Smoothie	Creamy Chicken Soup Orange Walnut Bark	Easy Creamy Pork Tenderloin
Day-4	Orange Walnut Bark	Cheesy Zucchini Manicotti	Baked Salmon Steaks with Onion and Dill (Plan #7)
Day-5	Coconut Crepes	Baked Salmon Steaks with Onion and Dill (Plan #7)	Easy Creamy Pork Tenderloin
Day-6	Orange Walnut Bark	Creamy Chicken Soup	Cheesy Zucchini Manicotti
Day-7	Coconut Crepes	Easy Creamy Pork Tenderloin	Creamy Chicken Soup Orange Walnut Bark

Shopping List

* 1½ lbs pork tenderloin
* 1 lb prosciutto
* Chicken broth
* 1 large chicken breast
* Frozen strawberries
* Plain Greek yogurt
* One can unsweetened almond milk
* Eggs
* Heavy whipping cream

* 4 zucchinis
* Onions
* Red bell peppers
* Fresh oregano
* Chicken broth
* Sage
* Parsley
* Orange extract

Almond Milk and Avocado Smoothie

Coconut Crepes

Cheesy Zucchini Manicotti

Creamy Chicken Soup

Recipe 1 (Breakfast): Almond Milk and Avocado Smoothie | Fat 59% | Protein 18% | Carbs 23%

Makes: 2 servings **Prep time:** 15 minutes **Store:** In an airtight container in the fridge for up to 4 days or in the freezer for up to 1 month.

1 cup avocados, cubed
½ cup plain Greek yogurt
¼ cup almond milk, unsweetened
½ tbsp. whey protein powder, unsweetened
1 tbsp. chopped walnuts

1. Blend the avocados in a blender until it has a smooth consistency.
2. Add the yogurt, almond milk, and protein powder, then process for another 2 minutes.
3. Separate the mixture into 2 bowls. Top with the walnuts and serve.

SERVE IT WITH: To make this a complete meal, serve with healthy keto green smoothie.

PER SERVING
calories: 140 | fat: 9.0g | total carbs: 6.0g | fiber: 1.8g | protein: 10.5g

Recipe 2 (Breakfast): Coconut Crepes | Fat 82% | Protein 11% | Carbs 7%

Makes: 2 servings **Prep time:** 5 minutes **Store:** In an airtight container in the fridge for up to 4 days or in the freezer for up to 1 month.

2 whisked eggs
½ cup heavy whipping cream
1 tsp. Swerve
2 tbsps. coconut flour
2 tbsps. melted coconut oil, divided
Sea salt, to taste

1. Mix 1 tbsp. coconut oil, eggs, salt, and Swerve in a bowl, then stir well to combine.
2. Add the coconut flour and cream until the mixture is smooth.
3. In a skillet, heat the remaining oil over medium heat. Pout half of the mixture into the skillet. Cook for 2 minutes on each side and repeat the process with the remaining mixture.
4. Remove from the heat and serve hot.

REHEAT: Microwave, covered, until it reaches the desired temperature.
SERVE IT WITH: To make this a complete meal, serve with keto cinnamon smoothie.

PER SERVING
calories: 390 | fat: 35.3g | total carbs: 7.4g | fiber: 0g | protein: 10.6g

Recipe 3 (Lunch/Dinner): Cheesy Zucchini Manicotti | Fat 76% | Protein 20% | Carbs 4%

Makes: 4 servings **Prep time:** 15 minutes **Store:** In an airtight container in the fridge for 3 to 5 days.

4 zucchinis, cut lengthwise into ⅛-inch-thick slices
Olive oil cooking spray
FILLING:
1 cup shredded Mozzarella cheese
1 cup goat cheese
½ cup grated Parmesan cheese
½ onion, minced
2 cups low-carb marinara sauce, divided
1 red bell pepper, diced
2 tsps. minced garlic
1 tbsp. chopped fresh oregano
2 tbsps. olive oil
Sea salt, to taste
Freshly ground black pepper, to taste

1. Preheat the oven to 375°F (190ºC). Grease a baking dish with olive oil cooking spray.
2. Make the filling: In a nonstick skillet, heat the olive oil over medium-high heat. Add the onion, garlic, and red bell pepper and sauté for 4 minutes, stirring occasionally.
3. Transfer the filling to a large bowl, add the Mozzarella cheese, goat cheese, oregano, salt and pepper, and mix well.
4. Make the manicotti: Pour 1 cup of marinara sauce in the baking dish and tilt pan to evenly distribute across the bottom. Put a slice of zucchini on a work surface, add a few tbsps. of the filling. Roll up and arrange on the baking dish, seam-side down. Repeat with the remaining zucchini slices.
5. Scatter the Parmesan cheese on top of each manicotti. Bake in the preheated oven for 30 minutes.
6. Transfer to a platter. Drizzle with the remaining marinara sauce and serve.

REHEAT: Microwave, covered, until the desired temperature is reached or reheat in a frying pan or instant pot, covered, on medium.
SERVE IT WITH: To make this dish complete, you can serve it with a crispy salad on the side.

PER SERVING
calories: 358 | fat: 30.2g | total carbs: 5.0g | fiber: 1.2g | protein: 17.8g

Recipe 4 (Lunch/Dinner): Easy Creamy Pork Tenderloin | Fat 50% | Protein 48% | Carbs 2%

Makes: 4 servings **Prep time:** 15 minutes **Store:** In a sealed airtight container in the fridge for up to 3 days or in your freezer for about 1 month.

1½ pounds (680 g) pork tenderloin, cut into ½-inch strips	2 tbsps. olive oil
	2 tbsps. fresh sage, chopped
¼ cup onion, chopped	2 tbsps. sun-dried tomatoes, chopped
¼ cup prosciutto, chopped	
½ cup heavy cream	2 tbsps. fresh parsley, chopped
½ cup chicken broth	¼ tsp. salt

1. Heat the oil in a suitable skillet over medium-high heat. Add the sage, tomatoes, parsley, onion, and prosciutto.
2. Cook for 5 minutes, then add the pork tenderloin strips to sear for 5 minutes per side.
3. Add the heavy cream, broth, and salt. Bring the gravy to a boil, then reduce the heat to low. Cook for 20 minutes, stirring occasionally. Serve hot.

REHEAT: Microwave, covered, until the desired temperature is reached or reheat in a frying pan or instant pot, covered, on medium.
SERVE IT WITH: To add more flavors to this meal, serve the pork tenderloin with asparagus bacon salad.

PER SERVING
calories: 330 | fat: 18.2g | total carbs: 2.8g | fiber: 0.7g | protein: 39.5g

Recipe 5 (Lunch/Dinner): Creamy Chicken Soup | Fat 83% | Protein 16% | Carbs 1%

Makes: 4 servings **Prep time:** 10 minutes **Store:** In an airtight container in the fridge for up to 2 days or in the freezer for up to 1 month.

4 ounces (113 g) cream cheese, cubed	½ cup heavy cream
	2 tbsps. Garlic Gusto Seasoning
14½ ounces (411 g) chicken broth	2 tbsps. butter
1 large chicken breast cut into strips	Salt, to taste

1. Melt butter in a saucepan over medium heat.
2. Add chicken strips and sauté for 2 minutes.
3. Add cream cheese and seasoning, and cook for 3

minutes, stirring occasionally.
4. Add the heavy cream and chicken broth. Heat until boiling, then reduce the heat.
5. Simmer for 4 minutes, then season with salt.
6. Remove from the heat. Allow to cool for 5 minutes before serving.

REHEAT: Microwave, covered, until the desired temperature is reached or reheat in a slow cooker or instant pot, covered, on medium.
SERVE IT WITH: To make this a complete meal, serve the garlicky chicken soup with roasted green beans on the side.

PER SERVING
calories: 243 | fat: 22.5g | total carbs: 7.0g | fiber: 6.6g | protein: 9.6g

Recipe 6 (Snack): Orange Walnut Bark | Fat 96% | Protein 3% | Carbs 1%

Makes: 6 servings **Prep time:** 15 minutes **Store:** It will remain fresh for about two weeks in the refrigerator and up to 2 months in a freezer.

⅔ cup raw walnut pieces, roasted	½ tsp. vanilla extract
	1¾ tsps. ground cardamom
¾ cup melted coconut oil	
⅛ tsp. finely ground gray sea salt	2 tsps. ginger powder
	2 tbsps. Erythritol
½ tsp. orange extract	

1. Pour all the ingredients in a food processor, except for the walnuts, pulse for 20 seconds.
2. Pulse the crushed walnuts in the food processor until walnut is about ¼ inch in size.
3. Pour the mixture into a parchment-lined square baking pan, and put it in the refrigerator for about an hour.
4. Take out the frozen mixture and break it into six pieces. Enjoy.

SERVE IT WITH: You can enjoy the barks as a snack with plain Greek yogurt or unsweetened coffee.

PER SERVING
calories: 336 | fat: 35.8g | total carbs: 2.4g | fiber: 1.1g | protein: 2.1g

Appendix 1: Measurement Conversion Chart

Volume Equivalents (Dry)

US STANDARD	METRIC (APPROXIMATE)
1/8 teaspoon	0.5 mL
1/4 teaspoon	1 mL
1/2 teaspoon	2 mL
3/4 teaspoon	4 mL
1 teaspoon	5 mL
1 tablespoon	15 mL
1/4 cup	59 mL
1/2 cup	118 mL
3/4 cup	177 mL
1 cup	235 mL
2 cups	475 mL
3 cups	700 mL
4 cups	1 L

Temperatures Equivalents

FAHRENHEIT (F)	CELSIUS(C) (APPROXIMATE)
225 °F	107 °C
250 °F	120 °C
275 °F	135 °C
300 °F	150 °C
325 °F	160 °C
350 °F	180 °C
375 °F	190 °C
400 °F	205 °C
425 °F	220 °C
450 °F	235 °C
475 °F	245 °C
500 °F	260 °C

Volume Equivalents (Liquid)

US STANDARD	US STANDARD (OUNCES)	METRIC (APPROXIMATE)
2 tablespoons	1 fl.oz.	30 mL
1/4 cup	2 fl.oz.	60 mL
1/2 cup	4 fl.oz.	120 mL
1 cup	8 fl.oz.	240 mL
1 1/2 cup	12 fl.oz.	355 mL
2 cups or 1 pint	16 fl.oz.	475 mL
4 cups or 1 quart	32 fl.oz.	1 L
1 gallon	128 fl.oz.	4 L

Weight Equivalents

US STANDARD	METRIC (APPROXIMATE)
1 ounce	28 g
2 ounces	57 g
5 ounces	142 g
10 ounces	284 g
15 ounces	425 g
16 ounces (1 pound)	455 g
1.5 pounds	680 g
2 pounds	907 g

Appendix 2: Recipes Index